JAVA

Modern Practices and Patterns

by Edson L P Camacho

Dedication and Gratitude

I extend my heartfelt gratitude to the following individuals who have played an essential role in the creation of this work:

1. **God**: At the forefront of my dedication, I express my profound thanks to the divine presence that guides and inspires me.

2. **My Family**:

    - **Wife Vanessa**: Your unwavering support and encouragement have been my anchor throughout this journey.
    - **Son Giovanni**: Your presence brings joy and motivation to my endeavors.
    - **Mother Maria**: Your wisdom and love have shaped me profoundly.
    - **Sisters Elaine and Elizete**: Your constant belief in my abilities has fueled my determination.

3. **Passionate Technologists**:

    - This work is dedicated to all those who share my enthusiasm for the ever-evolving world of technology. May our collective passion continue to drive progress and innovation.

With heartfelt appreciation,

Edson Camacho

Table of Contents

○ **Effective Java: Modern Practices and Patterns**

In the ever-evolving landscape of software development, mastering the art of writing efficient, reliable, and maintainable code is paramount. **Effective Java** has been a trusted guide for Java developers since its inception, and this new edition continues that legacy.

Overview:

In this book, we delve into the intricacies of Java, exploring both timeless principles and contemporary best practices. Whether you're a seasoned developer or just starting your journey, these pages offer valuable insights and actionable advice.

Key Topics Covered:

1. **Introduction to Effective Java**:

   - Understand the purpose and structure of this book.
   - Learn why effective Java programming matters in today's fast-paced world.

2. **Java Language Evolution**:

   - Navigate the changes that have occurred since the last edition (2008).
   - Explore the features introduced in Java 7 and Java 8.
   - Grasp the impact of Lambda expressions, streams, and generics on modern Java development.

3. **Design Patterns and Idioms**:

   - Discover new design patterns that have emerged since the second edition.
   - Master language idioms that enhance code readability and maintainability.
   - Apply these patterns to real-world scenarios.

4. **Functional Programming in Java**:

   - Dive into functional interfaces and their role in Java's evolution.
   - Harness the power of Lambda expressions for concise and expressive code.
   - Understand the benefits and potential pitfalls of functional programming.

5. **Collections and Streams**:

   - Leverage the Java Stream API for efficient bulk data operations.
   - Learn best practices for working with collections.
   - Transform and filter data effectively.

6. **Concurrency and Parallelism**:

   - Explore the improved Concurrency API.
   - Safeguard thread safety and synchronization.
   - Optimize your use of java.util.concurrent constructs.

7. **Java Time API**:

- Get acquainted with the new time-related classes.
- Handle dates, times, and time zones seamlessly.

8. **Serialization and Deserialization**:

- Follow best practices for object serialization.
- Avoid common pitfalls.
- Customize serialization/deserialization techniques.

9. **Common Mistakes and How to Avoid Them**:

- Uncover pitfalls related to equals, hashCode, and toString methods.
- Embrace defensive programming practices.
- Tackle null values and references effectively.

10. **Effective Code Organization and Libraries**:

- Learn strategies for structuring classes and packages.
- Maximize the use of java.lang and java.util.
- Tap into third-party libraries to enhance your Java projects.

May this edition of **Effective Java** empower you to write code that not only runs but also thrives in the dynamic world of software development. Let's embark on this journey together!

Happy coding,

Your Author

◦ Best Practices for Classes and Interfaces

Minimizing Accessibility of Classes and Members

In the realm of software design, **access control** plays a crucial role in maintaining a robust and maintainable codebase. By carefully managing the visibility of classes and their members, we can enhance encapsulation, reduce coupling, and promote good design practices. Let's explore why minimizing accessibility matters and how to achieve it effectively.

The Importance of Access Control

1. **Encapsulation and Information Hiding**:

   - **Encapsulation** is a fundamental principle in object-oriented programming. It involves bundling data (attributes) and methods (behavior) together within a class.
   - By restricting access to certain members, we hide implementation details from external code. This shields the internal workings of a class, preventing unintended interference.
   - Well-encapsulated classes are easier to reason about, maintain, and evolve.

2. **Reducing Coupling**:

   - **Coupling** refers to the degree of interdependence between different parts of a system.
   - When classes expose too much of their internals (e.g., public fields), they become tightly coupled to other classes. Changes in one class may ripple through dependent classes, leading to fragility.
   - Minimizing accessibility reduces coupling, allowing classes to evolve independently.

3. **API Design and Contracts**:

   - Public members form the contract between a class and its users. They define how external code interacts with the class.
   - Exposing only essential methods and hiding implementation details ensures a stable and well-defined API.
   - Changes to non-public members won't break existing code that relies on the public contract.

Strategies for Minimizing Accessibility

1. **Use Access Modifiers Wisely**:

   - Java provides access modifiers like public, protected, package-private (default), and private.
   - **Public**: Use sparingly. Only expose what's necessary for external use.
   - **Protected**: Limited use. Typically for inheritance scenarios.

- **Package-Private (Default)**: Use within the same package. Avoid exposing outside the package.
- **Private**: Restrict to the class itself. Hide implementation details.

2. **Accessor Methods Over Public Fields**:

   - Instead of exposing fields directly, use accessor methods (getters and setters).
   - Benefits:
     - Allows validation and control over data access.
     - Enables future changes (e.g., adding validation logic) without breaking existing code.
     - Encourages encapsulation.

3. **Immutable Classes**:

   - Immutable classes have read-only state. Fields are set during construction and remain unchanged.
   - Immutable objects are inherently thread-safe and promote better design.
   - Make fields final and avoid mutability wherever possible.

4. **Composition Over Inheritance**:

   - Favor composition (combining smaller components) over inheritance (extending base classes).
   - Inheritance exposes inherited members, potentially widening accessibility.
   - Composition allows fine-grained control over what's visible.

Minimizing accessibility isn't about being overly restrictive; it's about striking the right balance. Aim for clear contracts, encapsulation, and loose coupling. By doing so, you'll create classes that are easier to understand, maintain, and extend.

Remember: **Less is often more when it comes to access control.**

Effective Use of Access Modifiers in Java

Access modifiers in Java allow you to control the visibility and accessibility of classes, methods, and fields. Choosing the right access level is essential for maintaining a well-designed, encapsulated codebase. Let's explore how to use these modifiers effectively and provide examples of their impact on encapsulation and maintainability.

Access Modifiers Overview

1. **private**:

   - The most restrictive access level.
   - Members marked as private are accessible only within the same class.

- Example:

```
public class BankAccount {
    private double balance;

    public void deposit(double amount) {
        // Implementation details
    }
}
```

2. **package-private (Default)**:

- No explicit access modifier (i.e., no public, private, or protected).
- Members are accessible within the same package.
- Example:

```
class HelperClass {
    // Package-private field
    int count;

    // Package-private method
    void process() {
        // Implementation details
    }
}
```

3. **protected**:

- Members are accessible within the same package and by subclasses (even if they are in different packages).
- Useful for providing controlled access to subclasses.
- Example:

```
package com.example;

public class Vehicle {
    protected String make;

    protected void startEngine() {
        // Implementation details
    }
}
```

4. **public**:

- Least restrictive access level.
- Members are accessible from any class.

- Use with caution to expose essential parts of your API.
- Example:

```
public class Calculator {
  public double add(double a, double b) {
    // Implementation details
  }
}
```

Encapsulation and Maintainability

1. **Encapsulation Benefits**:

   - **Information Hiding**: Restricting access prevents direct manipulation of internal state. Clients interact through well-defined interfaces (public methods).
   - **Predictable Behavior**: Encapsulated classes are less prone to unintended side effects.
   - **Easier Refactoring**: Changes to internal implementation don't affect external code.

2. **Examples**:

   - **Minimizing Accessibility**:

     - Suppose we have a Person class with a private field for age. By keeping it private, we ensure that age can only be modified through appropriate methods (e.g., setAge() with validation).
     - This encapsulation prevents external code from directly altering the age, maintaining consistency.

   - **Package-Private for Helper Classes**:

     - Consider utility classes or helper methods that should only be used within a package.
     - By using package-private access, we limit their exposure to external classes, reducing the risk of misuse.

   - **Protected for Extensibility**:

     - In a base class, use protected for methods or fields that should be accessible to subclasses.
     - For instance, a Vehicle class may have a protected method startEngine(), allowing subclasses (e.g., Car, Motorcycle) to customize engine behavior.

   - **Public API Design**:

     - Public methods define your class's contract. Choose them carefully.
     - For example, a DatabaseConnection class should expose only necessary methods (e.g., connect(), executeQuery()), hiding low-level details.

Access modifiers are powerful tools for achieving encapsulation and maintaining code quality. Use them judiciously to strike the right balance between visibility and control. Remember that well-designed APIs enhance developer productivity and code reliability.

○ Using Accessor Methods in Public Classes

When designing public classes, it's essential to carefully consider how you expose your class members (fields and methods). While it may be tempting to directly expose public fields, doing so can lead to several drawbacks. Let's explore why accessor methods (also known as getters and setters) are a better choice and how they enhance encapsulation and maintainability.

Drawbacks of Exposing Public Fields

1. **Lack of Control**:

   - When you declare a field as public, any external code can directly modify its value. There's no control over how the field is accessed or modified.
   - Changes to the field's representation or validation logic become challenging because you can't intercept or validate assignments.

2. **Breaking Encapsulation**:

   - Encapsulation is the practice of bundling data (fields) and behavior (methods) together within a class.
   - Exposing fields directly breaks encapsulation by allowing external code to manipulate internal state without going through well-defined methods.

3. **Maintenance Challenges**:

   - Suppose you expose a public field, and later you need to add validation or additional behavior when setting its value.
   - You'll have to update all external code that directly accesses the field, which can be error-prone and time-consuming.

Benefits of Accessor Methods

1. **Encapsulation and Abstraction**:

   - Accessor methods provide an abstraction layer between the external world and the internal state of your class.
   - By using getters and setters, you define a clear contract for accessing and modifying data. Clients interact with the class through these methods, not directly with fields.

2. **Validation and Consistency**:

   - With accessor methods, you can enforce validation rules when setting values.
   - For example, a setAge(int age) method can ensure that the age is within a valid range (e.g., positive and not exceeding a maximum).

3. **Flexibility for Future Changes**:

   - Suppose you initially expose a field directly but later need to add logging or trigger some other action when the field changes.

- By using accessor methods from the start, you can seamlessly introduce such behavior without affecting existing code.

Example: Using Accessor Methods

Consider a Person class with an age field:

```
public class Person {
  private int age;

  public int getAge() {
    return age;
  }

  public void setAge(int age) {
    if (age >= 0 && age <= 120) {
      this.age = age;
    } else {
      throw new IllegalArgumentException("Invalid age value");
    }
  }
}
```

In this example:

- The getAge() method provides controlled access to the age field.
- The setAge(int age) method ensures that the age is valid (between 0 and 120).

By using accessor methods, you maintain encapsulation, improve code readability, and allow for future enhancements without breaking existing code.

Remember: **Accessor methods are your gateway to well-designed, maintainable classes. Choose them wisely!**

○ **Minimizing Mutability: The Power of Immutability**

In the world of software design, the concept of **immutability** holds significant importance. An immutable object is one that cannot be changed after it is created. Let's delve into what immutability means, explore its benefits, and understand how to design robust, immutable classes and methods.

What Is Immutability?

- **Immutability** refers to the property of an object that prevents it from being modified once it is created.
- In an immutable object:
  - The state (values of fields) remains constant throughout its lifetime.
  - Any operation on the object results in a new object with the desired changes, leaving the original object unchanged.

Benefits of Immutability

1. **Predictable Behavior**:

   - Immutable objects exhibit consistent behavior because their state doesn't change unexpectedly.
   - This predictability simplifies reasoning about code and debugging.
2. **Thread Safety**:

   - Immutable objects are inherently thread-safe.
   - Since they cannot be modified, there are no race conditions or synchronization issues.
3. **Enhanced Security**:

   - Immutable objects cannot be tampered with once created.
   - This property is valuable in scenarios like cryptographic algorithms or secure data structures.
4. **Stable APIs**:

   - Public APIs should ideally use immutable objects.
   - Once an API is defined, changes to the underlying implementation won't affect existing clients.

Scenarios Where Mutability Causes Issues

1. **Shared State**:

   - Mutable objects shared among multiple threads can lead to race conditions.
   - Concurrent modifications can result in unexpected behavior.
2. **Caching and Memoization**:

   - Caching results in mutable objects can lead to stale data.

- Immutable caches avoid this issue.

3. **Collections and Hashing**:

- Mutable objects in collections can cause problems when used as keys in hash-based data structures.
- If an object's hash code changes after being added to a collection, it becomes inaccessible.

Guidelines for Designing Immutable Classes

1. **Make Fields final**:

- Declare fields as final to prevent modification after construction.
- Initialize them in the constructor.

2. **No Setter Methods**:

- Avoid providing setter methods for fields.
- If modification is necessary, create a new object with the desired changes.

3. **Return Copies of Mutable Objects**:

- If a field contains a mutable object (e.g., a list), return a copy to prevent external modifications.
- Defensive copying ensures immutability.

4. **Avoid Mutable State in Constructors**:

- Ensure that constructors don't modify shared state.
- Initialize fields directly or with immutable values.

Example of an Immutable Class:

```
public final class Point {
   private final int x;
   private final int y;

   public Point(int x, int y) {
      this.x = x;
      this.y = y;
   }

   public int getX() {
      return x;
   }

   public int getY() {
      return y;
   }
}
```

In this example, the Point class is immutable. Once created, its coordinates (x and y) cannot change.

Remember: **Immutability promotes stability, reliability, and better code quality. Choose it wisely!**

○ **Favoring Composition Over Inheritance: A Design Paradigm**

In the realm of object-oriented programming (OOP), two fundamental approaches shape class relationships: **inheritance** and **composition**. Each approach has distinct advantages and trade-offs. Let's explore these concepts, highlight their differences, and delve into the power of composition.

Inheritance vs. Composition

1. **Inheritance**:

   - **Is-a Relationship**: Inheritance models an "is-a" relationship between a base class (superclass) and its derived classes (subclasses).
   - **Code Reuse**: Subclasses inherit the state and behavior of the superclass.
   - **Drawbacks**:
     - Tight coupling: Changes in the superclass affect all subclasses.
     - Limited flexibility: Subclasses are bound to the base class's implementation.

2. **Composition**:

   - **Has-a Relationship**: Composition represents a "has-a" relationship between classes.
   - **Component-Based**: A class contains instances of other classes (components) as fields.
   - **Benefits**:
     - Flexibility: Components can change independently.
     - Reusability: Components can be reused in different contexts.

Flexibility and Reusability

1. **Composition's Flexibility**:

   - By composing classes, you create modular components that can evolve independently.
   - Example: A Car class composed of an Engine, Wheels, and Chassis. You can replace or upgrade individual components without affecting the entire car.

2. **Reusability Through Composition**:

   - Composition allows you to reuse existing classes without inheriting their implementation.
   - Example: A Person class composed of a Name, Address, and ContactInfo. These components can be reused in other contexts (e.g., Employee, Customer).

Composing Classes Using Interfaces and Delegation

1. **Interfaces**:

   - Define contracts (method signatures) that classes must implement.
   - Use interfaces to compose behavior.
   - Example: A Drawable interface for objects that can be drawn on a canvas.

2. **Delegation**:

   - Delegate responsibility to other objects.
   - Example: A Logger class delegates logging tasks to an internal LogWriter.

Example: Composition with Interfaces

Consider a drawing application:

```
interface Drawable {
   void draw();
}

class Circle implements Drawable {
   // Circle-specific implementation
   public void draw() {
      // Draw a circle
   }
}

class Square implements Drawable {
   // Square-specific implementation
   public void draw() {
      // Draw a square
   }
}

class Canvas {
   private final List<Drawable> shapes = new ArrayList<>();

   public void addShape(Drawable shape) {
      shapes.add(shape);
   }

   public void render() {
      for (Drawable shape : shapes) {
         shape.draw();
      }
   }
}
```

In this example:

- Circle and Square implement the Drawable interface.
- The Canvas class composes shapes using a list of Drawable instances.
- The render() method delegates drawing to each shape.

Composition promotes flexibility, reusability, and maintainability. Use it wisely to create modular, extensible systems. Remember: **"Favor composition over inheritance."**

○ Static Factory Methods vs. Constructors

Introduction

When designing Java classes, one of the fundamental decisions is how to allow clients (other parts of your code) to create instances of those classes. Traditionally, we use **constructors** for this purpose.

However, there's another powerful technique that should be part of every programmer's toolkit: **static factory methods**.

In this article, we'll explore the differences between constructors and static factory methods, their advantages, and when to use each approach.

Constructors

1. **What Are Constructors?**

   - Constructors are special methods within a class that initialize objects when they are created.
   - They have the same name as the class and are called using the new keyword.
   - Constructors can be overloaded to accept different parameters.

2. **Drawbacks of Constructors:**

   - Constructors don't always provide clear semantics. Their names are often limited to the class name, which might not convey their purpose effectively.
   - Overloaded constructors can lead to confusion, especially when there are many variations.

Static Factory Methods

1. **What Are Static Factory Methods?**

   - A **static factory method** is a static method within a class that returns an instance of that class.
   - Unlike constructors, static factory methods can have meaningful names that describe their purpose.
   - They allow you to encapsulate object creation logic and provide a more expressive API.

2. **Advantages of Static Factory Methods:**

   - **Clear Naming:**

     - Static factory methods can have descriptive names, making it easier for clients to understand their purpose.
     - Example: Boolean.valueOf(boolean b) creates a Boolean object from a boolean primitive value.

   - **Caching and Reuse:**

     - Static factory methods can cache instances and return them if needed.
     - This can improve performance by reusing existing objects instead of creating new ones.

   - **Flexibility:**

- Static factory methods allow you to return subtypes or different implementations based on input parameters.
- Constructors, on the other hand, always return an instance of the exact class.

- **Privacy Control:**

  - You can make constructors private and provide static factory methods as the only way to create instances.
  - Useful for enforcing certain rules or managing resource allocation.

3. **Example: Creating a List**

```
// Using a constructor
List<String> myList = new ArrayList<>(); // Less expressive

// Using a static factory method
List<String> newList = new ArrayList<>(myList); // More expressive
```

Static factory methods offer flexibility, better naming, and control over object creation. While constructors remain essential, consider using static factory methods when designing your classes. They enhance code readability and provide a cleaner API for clients.

Remember Joshua Bloch's advice from his book "Effective Java": **"Consider static factory methods instead of constructors."**

○ **The Challenge of Many Constructor Parameters**

Imagine a scenario where you're designing a class to represent **Nutrition Facts labels** found on packaged foods. These labels have a few **required fields** (such as serving size, servings per container, and calories per serving) and **over twenty optional fields** (like total fat, saturated fat, trans fat, cholesterol, sodium, etc.). Most products have nonzero values for only a few of these optional fields.

Traditionally, programmers have used the **telescoping constructor pattern**, which involves providing constructors with varying numbers of parameters. However, this approach doesn't scale well when the number of optional parameters increases. Let's take a look at how it might look in practice:

```java
// Telescoping constructor pattern - does not scale well!
public class NutritionFacts {
    private final int servingSize;    // (mL)            required
    private final int servings;       // (per container) required
    private final int calories;       //                 optional
    private final int fat;            // (g)             optional
    private final int sodium;         // (mg)            optional
    private final int carbohydrate;   // (g)             optional

    public NutritionFacts(int servingSize, int servings) {
        this(servingSize, servings, 0);
    }

    public NutritionFacts(int servingSize, int servings, int calories) {
        this(servingSize, servings, calories, 0);
    }

    // ... more constructors for additional optional parameters ...

    public NutritionFacts(int servingSize, int servings, int calories, int fat, int sodium, int carbohydrate) {
        this.servingSize = servingSize;
        this.servings = servings;
        this.calories = calories;
        this.fat = fat;
        this.sodium = sodium;
        this.carbohydrate = carbohydrate;
    }
}
```

When creating an instance, you're forced to pass values for all parameters, even if you don't want to set them. For example:

```java
NutritionFacts cocaCola = new NutritionFacts(240, 8, 100, 0, 35, 27);
```

As you can see, this approach becomes unwieldy as the number of parameters grows.

◦ **The Builder Pattern to the Rescue**

Enter the **builder pattern**! Instead of relying solely on constructors, consider using a builder to create instances of your class. Here's how it works:

1. Create an inner static class (the builder) within your main class.
2. The builder class has methods for setting each parameter.
3. The builder returns itself after each method call, allowing for method chaining.
4. Finally, the builder provides a method to build the actual object.

Let's refactor our NutritionFacts class using the builder pattern:

```java
public class NutritionFacts {
   private final int servingSize;
   private final int servings;
   private final int calories;
   private final int fat;
   private final int sodium;
   private final int carbohydrate;

   public static class Builder {
      private final int servingSize;
      private final int servings;
      private int calories = 0;
      private int fat = 0;
      private int sodium = 0;
      private int carbohydrate = 0;

      public Builder(int servingSize, int servings) {
         this.servingSize = servingSize;
         this.servings = servings;
      }

      public Builder calories(int calories) {
         this.calories = calories;
         return this;
      }

      public Builder fat(int fat) {
         this.fat = fat;
         return this;
      }

      // ... more methods for other optional parameters ...

       public NutritionFacts build() {
         return new NutritionFacts(this);
      }
   }

   private NutritionFacts(Builder builder) {
```

```
        this.servingSize = builder.servingSize;
        this.servings = builder.servings;
        this.calories = builder.calories;
        this.fat = builder.fat;
        this.sodium = builder.sodium;
        this.carbohydrate = builder.carbohydrate;
    }
}
```

Now, creating an instance is more expressive and flexible:

```
NutritionFacts cocaCola = new NutritionFacts.Builder(240, 8)
    .calories(100)
    .sodium(35)
    .carbohydrate(27)
    .build();
```

The builder pattern allows you to set only the parameters you need, resulting in cleaner code and better readability.

Remember: **Consider a builder when faced with many constructor parameters!**

○ Singleton Design Pattern

The **singleton pattern** ensures that a class has only one instance and provides a global point of access to that instance. It is commonly used for scenarios where a single instance needs to coordinate actions across the system.

1. Private Constructor Approach

In the traditional approach, you enforce the singleton property by making the constructor private. Here's how it works:

```
public class MySingleton {
    private static final MySingleton INSTANCE = new MySingleton();

    // Private constructor prevents instantiation from other classes
    private MySingleton() {
        // Initialization code (if needed)
    }

    public static MySingleton getInstance() {
        return INSTANCE;
    }
}
```

- The INSTANCE field is a static final variable that holds the single instance of MySingleton.
- The private constructor ensures that no other class can create additional instances.
- Clients access the singleton instance via the getInstance() method.

2. Enum Type Approach

An elegant and thread-safe way to implement a singleton is by using an **enum type**. Enum constants are implicitly static and final, making them suitable for singletons:

```
public enum MySingleton {
    INSTANCE;

    // Additional methods or fields (if needed)
}
```

- The INSTANCE enum constant represents the singleton instance.
- Enums guarantee that there is only one instance of each enum constant.
- Enums handle serialization and thread safety automatically.

Advantages of Enum Approach:

1. **Thread Safety:**

    - Enum instances are inherently thread-safe.
    - No need to worry about synchronization or double-checked locking.

2. **Serialization Safety:**

    - Enums handle serialization and deserialization consistently.
    - Singleton properties are preserved during serialization.

3. **Clarity and Readability:**

    - Enum-based singletons are concise and self-explanatory.
    - No need for additional methods or fields.

Both approaches enforce the singleton property effectively.

Remember: **Choose wisely based on your specific requirements**, but consider using enums for singletons whenever possible.

• Enforcing Noninstantiability with a Private Constructor

1. **Why Enforce Noninstantiability?**

   - Some classes are not meant to be instantiated (e.g., utility classes with only static methods or classes holding constants).
   - Preventing instantiation ensures that the class serves its purpose without unnecessary object creation.

2. **Private Constructor Approach:**

   - Declare a **private constructor** within the class.
   - Since the constructor is private, no other class can create instances of it.
   - The default constructor (with no arguments) won't be generated automatically.

3. **Example: String Constants Class**

```
public final class MyStrings {
   // Private constructor prevents instantiation
   private MyStrings() {
      // Optional: Initialization code (if needed)
   }

   public static final String ONE = "something";
   public static final String TWO = "another";
   // ... other constants ...

   // Additional methods (if needed)
}
```

4. **Benefits:**

   - No performance or memory overhead from the private constructor.
   - Prevents inheritance because the superclass constructor cannot be called.
   - Clear intent: Users know not to instantiate this class.

5. **Alternative: Enum Type (if available)**

   - If you're using Java 5 or later, consider using an **enum type** for singletons or noninstantiable classes.
   - Enums handle serialization and thread safety automatically.

6. **Effective Java Wisdom:**

   - It's a clean and straightforward way to enforce noninstantiability.

Remember: **Private constructors are a powerful tool for creating utility classes or preventing unnecessary object creation.**

○ **Dependency Injection vs. Hardwiring Resources**

1. **Dependency Injection:**

   - **What is it?**
     - Dependency injection (DI) is a technique where a class's dependencies (such as other objects or resources) are provided from the outside.
     - Instead of creating dependencies within the class, we inject them during object creation.
   - **Advantages:**
     - **Flexibility:** DI allows you to change dependencies without modifying the class itself.
     - **Testability:** You can easily mock or substitute dependencies during unit testing.
     - **Readability:** The class's dependencies are explicitly declared in its constructor or methods.
   - **Example:**

```
public class DatabaseManager {
  private final DatabaseConfig config;

  public DatabaseManager(DatabaseConfig config) {
    this.config = config;
  }

  // Other methods that use the config...
}
```

2. **Hardwiring Resources:**

   - **What is it?**
     - Hardwiring resources means directly creating or initializing them within the class.
     - This approach tightly couples the class to specific resources.
   - **Drawbacks:**
     - **Inflexibility:** Changing resources requires modifying the class code.
     - **Testing Challenges:** Hardwired resources are difficult to mock during testing.
     - **Maintenance Burden:** Tracking and managing resource changes becomes complex.
   - **Example (Avoid This):**

```
public class HardwiredManager {
  private final DatabaseConfig config = new DatabaseConfig(); // Hardwired
  // Other methods that use the config...
}
```

3. **Effective Java Wisdom:**

   - Use constructor injection or setter injection to provide dependencies.
   - Frameworks like Spring and Guice simplify DI.

4. **Conclusion:**

   - **Prefer dependency injection** to allow flexibility, improve testability, and enhance code readability.
   - Avoid hardwiring resources directly within your classes.

Remember: **Design for maintainability and adaptability by embracing dependency injection!**

○ **Avoid Creating Unnecessary Objects**

1. **String Concatenation:**

   - Instead of repeatedly concatenating strings using the + operator, use StringBuilder or StringBuffer.
   - Example:

   ```
   // Inefficient:
   String result = "";
   for (int i = 0; i < 1000; i++) {
       result += i;
   }

   // Efficient:
   StringBuilder builder = new StringBuilder();
   for (int i = 0; i < 1000; i++) {
       builder.append(i);
   }
   String efficientResult = builder.toString();
   ```

2. **Autoboxing and Unboxing:**

   - Be cautious with autoboxing (automatic conversion between primitive types and their wrapper classes).
   - Explicitly use primitives when possible to avoid unnecessary object creation.
   - Example:

   ```
   // Inefficient:
   Integer sum = 0;
   for (int i = 1; i <= 1000; i++) {
       sum += i; // Autoboxing
   }

   // Efficient:
   int efficientSum = 0;
   for (int i = 1; i <= 1000; i++) {
       efficientSum += i;
   }
   ```

Eliminate Obsolete Object References

1. **Memory Leaks:**

   - Holding references to objects that are no longer needed can lead to memory leaks.
   - Explicitly set references to null when an object becomes obsolete.
   - Example:

   ```
   List<String> myList = new ArrayList<>();
   ```

```
// Use myList...
myList = null; // Mark as obsolete
```

2. **Garbage Collection:**

   - Java's garbage collector reclaims memory from unreachable objects.
   - However, objects with lingering references won't be garbage-collected.
   - Avoid keeping references longer than necessary.

3. **Caching and Pooling:**

   - Be cautious with caching and object pooling.
   - Clear cached objects when they are no longer needed.
   - Use libraries like Apache Commons Pool for efficient pooling.

Remember: **Efficient object management improves performance and reduces memory overhead.**

○ Finalizers

1. What Are Finalizers?

- Finalizers (also known as **finalize methods**) are special methods in Java that are called by the garbage collector before an object is reclaimed.
- They are defined using the finalize() method.

2. Drawbacks of Finalizers:

- **Unpredictable Execution:**
  - The timing of finalizer execution is not guaranteed.
  - Finalizers can run at an arbitrary point during garbage collection.
- **Performance Impact:**
  - Finalizers introduce overhead due to their execution.
  - They delay object reclamation.
- **Resource Leaks:**
  - If an object holds external resources (such as files, sockets, or database connections), finalizers may not release them promptly.
  - This can lead to resource leaks.

3. Alternatives to Finalizers:

- **Try-With-Resources:**
  - Use try-with-resources blocks to manage external resources.
  - Implement AutoCloseable or Closeable interfaces for resource management.
- **Explicit Cleanup Methods:**
  - Define explicit cleanup methods (e.g., close()) that clients can call explicitly.
  - Release resources immediately when the client is done using the object.

Cleaners (Java 9+)

1. What Are Cleaners?

- Cleaners are a replacement for finalizers introduced in Java 9.
- They allow you to register cleanup actions to be executed when an object becomes unreachable.
- Cleaners are more predictable than finalizers.

2. Cleaner Example:

```
public class MyResource implements AutoCloseable {
    private final Cleaner.Cleanable cleanable;

    public MyResource() {
        this.cleanable = Cleaner.create(this, () -> releaseResource());
```

3.

```
    }

    private void releaseResource() {
        // Release external resource here
    }

    @Override
    public void close() {
        cleanable.clean();
    }
}
```

4. **Advantages of Cleaners:**

- **Predictable Execution:**
    - Cleaners execute predictably when the object becomes unreachable.
- **Resource Management:**
    - Use cleaners to manage external resources.
    - They work well with try-with-resources.

Avoid finalizers whenever possible due to their drawbacks. Instead, use try-with-resources, explicit cleanup methods, or cleaners (if available).

Remember: **Explicit resource management leads to better code quality and fewer surprises.**

○ **Try-With-Resources vs. Try-Finally**

1. **Try-With-Resources:**

   - Introduced in Java 7, try-with-resources simplifies resource management.
   - It automatically closes resources (such as files, sockets, or database connections) when they are no longer needed.
   - Resources must implement the AutoCloseable or Closeable interface.
   - Example:

   ```
   try (FileInputStream fis = new FileInputStream("myfile.txt");
       BufferedReader reader = new BufferedReader(new InputStreamReader(fis))) {
       // Read from the file
   } catch (IOException e) {
       // Handle exceptions
   }
   ```

2. **Advantages of Try-With-Resources:**

   - **Automatic Cleanup:**
     - Resources are closed automatically at the end of the block.
   - **Readability:**
     - The code is concise and easier to read.
   - **Exception Handling:**
     - Exceptions thrown during resource closing are properly handled.

3. **Try-Finally (Pre-Java 7):**

   - In older Java versions, try-finally was the primary way to ensure resource cleanup.
   - It requires manual resource closing within the finally block.
   - Example:

   ```
   FileInputStream fis = null;
   try {
     fis = new FileInputStream("myfile.txt");
     // Read from the file
   } catch (IOException e) {
     // Handle exceptions
   } finally {
     if (fis != null) {
       try {
         fis.close();
       } catch (IOException e) {
         // Handle close exception
       }
     }
   }
   ```

- Always prefer try-with-resources for cleaner and safer resource management.
- Use try-finally only when working with older Java versions or non-AutoCloseable resources.

Remember: **Try-with-resources simplifies resource handling and reduces boilerplate code.**

○ **The important topic of overriding the equals method in Java.**

When you override this method, it's crucial to adhere to its general contract. Here are the key principles to keep in mind:

1. **Reflexive**: For any non-null reference value x, x.equals(x) must return true.
2. **Symmetric**: For any non-null reference values x and y, x.equals(y) must return true if and only if y.equals(x) returns true.
3. **Transitive**: If x.equals(y) and y.equals(z) are both true, then x.equals(z) must also be true.
4. **Consistent**: The result of x.equals(y) should remain the same if the values of x and y remain unchanged.

Now, let's explore an example of overriding the equals method in Java. Suppose we have a Person class with two fields: name (a String) and age (an int). We want to compare two Person objects based on these fields.

```java
public class Person {
    private String name;
    private int age;

    public Person(String name, int age) {
        this.name = name;
        this.age = age;
    }

    @Override
    public boolean equals(Object obj) {
        if (obj == null || getClass() != obj.getClass()) {
            return false;
        }

        final Person other = (Person) obj;
        return (this.name == null ? other.name == null : this.name.equals(other.name))
            && this.age == other.age;
    }

    @Override
    public int hashCode() {
        int hash = 3;
        hash = 53 * hash + (this.name != null ? this.name.hashCode() : 0);
        hash = 53 * hash + this.age;
        return hash;
    }

    // Getters and setters for age (not shown here)
}
```

In this example:

- We compare name using equals (which works for String).
- We use == to compare age because it's an int.

Remember that adhering to the general contract ensures consistent behavior when using collections (e.g., ArrayList, HashSet) and other Java classes that rely on equals and hashCode.

○ **When you override the equals method in Java**

It's essential to also override the hashCode method. These two methods are closely related, and adhering to this principle ensures consistent behavior when using collections (such as HashSet, HashMap, or Hashtable) that rely on both equals and hashCode.

Here's why you should always override hashCode when overriding equals:

1. **Consistency**: The hashCode method provides an integer value that represents the object's state. When two objects are equal (according to their equals method), their hash codes must be the same. Inconsistent hash codes can lead to unexpected behavior in hash-based collections.

2. **Hash-Based Collections**: Collections like HashSet and HashMap use hash codes to organize and retrieve elements efficiently. If you override equals without overriding hashCode, you risk violating the contract between these methods, leading to incorrect behavior in these collections.

3. **Performance**: Efficient hash codes distribute objects evenly across buckets in hash-based collections. If you don't override hashCode, the default implementation (which is based on memory addresses) may not provide good distribution, resulting in poor performance.

Here's an example of how to override both equals and hashCode for a Person class:

```
public class Person {
  private String name;
  private int age;

  public Person(String name, int age) {
    this.name = name;
    this.age = age;
  }

  @Override
  public boolean equals(Object obj) {
    if (obj == null || getClass() != obj.getClass()) {
      return false;
    }

    final Person other = (Person) obj;
    return (this.name == null ? other.name == null : this.name.equals(other.name))
        && this.age == other.age;
  }

  @Override
  public int hashCode() {
    int result = 17; // A prime number as the initial value
    result = 31 * result + (name != null ? name.hashCode() : 0);
    result = 31 * result + age;
    return result;
  }
}
```

```
    // Getters and setters for age (not shown here)
}
```

In this example:

- We use a prime number (17) as the initial value for the hash code.
- We combine the hash codes of the name field (using hashCode()) and the age field (directly).

Remember to test your equals and hashCode implementations thoroughly to ensure correctness and consistency.

○ **Overriding the toString method in Java**

Is essential for providing a meaningful and human-readable representation of an object. When you override toString, you customize how your class instances are displayed when converted to strings.

Here's how you can override the toString method in a class:

```java
public class Person {
    private String name;
    private int age;

    public Person(String name, int age) {
        this.name = name;
        this.age = age;
    }

    // Other methods and fields...

    @Override
    public String toString() {
        return "Person{" +
            "name='" + name + '\"' +
            ", age=" + age +
            '}';
    }

    // Getters and setters (not shown here)
}
```

In this example:

- We override toString to return a formatted string containing the person's name and age.
- The format "Person{name='John', age=30}" provides useful information for debugging and logging.

Remember to customize the toString output based on your class's properties and their significance. It's a helpful practice for debugging and improving code readability.

Let's delve into the topic of **overriding the clone method in Java judiciously**. The clone method allows you to create a copy of an object, but its usage requires careful consideration. We'll explore why you should override it thoughtfully and provide best practices.

- ○ **Why Override clone?**

1. **Object Cloning**:

   - The clone method creates a new object that is a copy of the original.
   - By default, it performs a shallow copy, meaning it copies references to the same objects rather than creating new instances of referenced objects.
   - Cloning is useful for scenarios like creating backups, prototypes, or avoiding concurrent modification issues.

2. **The General Contract**:

   - When you override clone, you must adhere to the general contract defined by Object.
   - The contract specifies that the cloned object should be equal to the original (according to equals), but they should not be the same object (i.e., obj != obj.clone()).

3. **Array Fields and Shallow Copy**:

   - Arrays are reference types, and a shallow copy of an array field in a class will share the same array between the original and the clone.
   - This can lead to unintended consequences if you modify the array in one instance, affecting the other.

Judiciously Overriding clone

1. **Implement Cloneable**:

   - To enable cloning, your class should implement the Cloneable interface.
   - However, it's recommended to avoid using Cloneable for new classes and prefer other approaches (e.g., copy constructors or factories).

2. **Override clone**:

   - When overriding clone, follow these guidelines:
     - Call super.clone() to create a shallow copy of the object.
     - Then, fix any mutable fields (like arrays) to ensure they are properly copied.
     - Avoid making the method public—it should be protected to prevent external misuse.

3. **Deep Copy for Array Fields**:

   - If your class contains an array field, you must perform a deep copy of that array in the clone method.

- Otherwise, both the original and the clone will refer to the same array, violating the contract.

4. **Example Implementation**:

   - Let's consider a Student class with a name, age, and an array of marks:

```java
public class Student implements Cloneable {
    private String name;
    private int age;
    private int[] marks = {90, 70, 80};

    @Override
    protected Student clone() throws CloneNotSupportedException {
        Student student = (Student) super.clone();
        student.marks = marks.clone(); // Perform a deep copy of the array
        return student;
    }

    // Other methods and fields...
}
```

   - In this example, we ensure that the marks array is correctly copied.

Overriding clone judiciously involves understanding the implications of shallow copying and ensuring that mutable fields are properly handled. Consider alternatives like copy constructors or factories when possible. By following best practices, you can use clone effectively and avoid unexpected behavior.

Remember, **judiciousness** is key!

○ **Implementing the Comparable interface**

Is a powerful way to provide natural ordering for objects of the same type. Let's explore how to use it effectively:

1. **What is Comparable?**

   - The Comparable interface defines a strategy for comparing an object with other objects of the same type.
   - By implementing Comparable, you enable your class instances to be compared and sorted based on their natural order.

2. **How to Implement Comparable?**

   - To make your class comparable, follow these steps:
     - Ensure your class implements the Comparable<T> interface, where T is the type of objects you want to compare.
     - Override the compareTo method, which compares the current instance with another instance of the same type.
     - The compareTo method should return a negative value if the current instance is less than the other, zero if they are equal, and a positive value if the current instance is greater.

3. **Example: Sorting Pairs**

   - Suppose we have a Pair class with two fields: x (a String) and y (an int).
   - We want to sort an array of Pair objects lexicographically by x and, if x values are the same, by their y values.
   - Here's an example implementation:

```java
import java.util.*;

class Pair implements Comparable<Pair> {
  String x;
  int y;

  public Pair(String x, int y) {
    this.x = x;
    this.y = y;
  }

  @Override
  public int compareTo(Pair other) {
    if (!this.x.equals(other.x)) {
      return this.x.compareTo(other.x);
    } else {
      return Integer.compare(this.y, other.y);
    }
  }

  public String toString() {
```

```java
      return "(" + x + "," + y + ")";
    }
}

public class Main {
    public static void main(String[] args) {
        Pair[] arr = {
            new Pair("abc", 3),
            new Pair("a", 4),
            new Pair("bc", 5),
            new Pair("a", 2)
        };

        Arrays.sort(arr);
        print(arr);
    }

    public static void print(Pair[] arr) {
        for (Pair p : arr) {
            System.out.println(p);
        }
    }
}
```

- Implementing Comparable allows your class to interoperate with generic algorithms and collections that rely on natural ordering.
- Remember to override compareTo thoughtfully based on your class's properties.

○ Java Design: Inheritance and Its Documentation

Inheritance is one of the four fundamental principles of Object-Oriented Programming (OOP). It allows a class to inherit the properties and methods of another class. In Java, this is achieved using the extends keyword.

The Power of Inheritance

Inheritance promotes code reusability and a logical structure for our programs. A class that inherits from another class (the superclass) can reuse methods and fields declared in the superclass, and it can also define its own unique behavior.

```
public class Animal {
   public void eat() {
      System.out.println("The animal eats");
   }
}

public class Dog extends Animal {
   public void bark() {
      System.out.println("The dog barks");
   }
}
```

In the above example, Dog is a subclass of Animal and inherits the eat method from Animal. It also defines an additional method bark.

Documenting Inheritance

When documenting your Java code, it's important to clearly indicate the relationships between your classes. Javadoc, the standard tool for generating API documentation in HTML format from Java source code, can help with this.

```
/**
 * The Animal class represents a general animal in the wild.
 */
public class Animal {
   /**
    * This method describes the eating behavior of the animal.
    */
   public void eat() {
      System.out.println("The animal eats");
   }
}

/**
 * The Dog class represents a specific animal - a dog.
 * It is a subclass of the Animal class and inherits all of its behaviors.
```

```
*/
public class Dog extends Animal {
  /**
   * This method describes the barking behavior of the dog.
   */
  public void bark() {
     System.out.println("The dog barks");
  }
}
```

Prohibiting Inheritance

In some cases, you might want to prevent a class from being subclassed. In Java, you can do this by marking the class with the final keyword.

```
public final class ImmutableClass {
  // class definition
}
```

In the above example, ImmutableClass cannot be subclassed.

Inheritance is a powerful feature in Java that promotes code reusability and a clear, logical structure. Proper documentation of inheritance relationships is crucial for understanding and maintaining your code. While inheritance is generally beneficial, there are cases where it may be necessary to prohibit it, which can be achieved using the final keyword.

Remember, good design and clear documentation are key to successful programming! Happy coding!

○ **Flexibility**

Java does not support multiple inheritance of classes, which means a class can only extend one other class. However, a class can implement multiple interfaces. This provides greater flexibility in designing your classes.

Loose Coupling

Interfaces provide a way to ensure that a class adheres to a certain contract without enforcing a strict hierarchy. This leads to a more loosely coupled and modular design, which is easier to read, maintain, and test.

Evolution of Interfaces

With the introduction of default methods in interfaces in Java 8, interfaces can now provide behavior, not just method signatures. This makes interfaces even more powerful and flexible.

Here's an example:

```java
interface Flyable {
   void fly();

   // Default method
   default void land() {
      System.out.println("Landing...");
   }
}

class Bird implements Flyable {
   @Override
   public void fly() {
      System.out.println("Flying...");
   }
}

class Plane implements Flyable {
   @Override
   public void fly() {
      System.out.println("Flying...");
   }

   // Override default method
   @Override
   public void land() {
      System.out.println("Plane is landing...");
   }
}
```

In this example, both Bird and Plane classes implement the Flyable interface and can define their own fly method. The land method is a default method in the interface, which can be overridden by any class that implements the interface.

Remember, while interfaces are powerful, the choice between interfaces and abstract classes will depend on your specific use case. It's always important to consider the needs of your design before making a decision.

Designing interfaces for posterity is an important aspect of software development. Here's a brief guide on how to do it:

○ Designing Interfaces for Posterity

1. Think About the Future

When designing an interface, consider how it might evolve in the future. Will new methods be added? Could it be implemented by different types of classes? Design your interface to be flexible and adaptable to future changes.

2. Keep It Simple

An interface should be as simple as possible. It should have a single responsibility and not try to do too much. This makes it easier to implement and understand.

```
public interface Vehicle {
    void drive();
}
```

3. Use Descriptive Names

The names of your interfaces and methods should clearly describe what they do. This makes your code easier to read and understand.

```
public interface PaymentProcessor {
    void processPayment(Payment payment);
}
```

4. Document Your Interfaces

Use Javadoc comments to document your interfaces. Explain what each method does, what parameters it takes, and what it returns. This will be invaluable for other developers who need to use or implement your interface.

```
/**
 * This interface represents a payment processor.
 * It defines a single method for processing payments.
 */
public interface PaymentProcessor {
    /**
     * Processes a payment.
     *
     * @param payment the payment to process
     */
    void processPayment(Payment payment);
```

}

5. Consider Using Default Methods

Java 8 introduced default methods, which allow you to add new methods to your interfaces without breaking existing implementations. This can be very useful when your interfaces need to evolve.

```java
public interface Vehicle {
    void drive();

    default void stop() {
        System.out.println("Vehicle stopped.");
    }
}
```

Remember, the goal of designing interfaces for posterity is to ensure that your interfaces remain useful and relevant, even as your software evolves.

Using interfaces solely to define types is a common practice in Java and many other object-oriented programming languages. This approach is often referred to as the "Interface Segregation Principle" (ISP), one of the five principles of SOLID.

- ○ **Interface Segregation Principle (ISP)**

The ISP states that no client should be forced to depend on interfaces they do not use. This means that an interface should not contain more functionality than a particular class needs.

Defining Types with Interfaces

When you use an interface to define a type, you're essentially defining a contract for what a class can do, without specifying how it does it. Here's an example:

```
public interface Drivable {
    void drive();
}
```

In this example, Drivable is an interface that defines a type of objects that can perform a drive operation. Any class that implements this interface must provide an implementation for the drive method.

```
public class Car implements Drivable {
    @Override
    public void drive() {
        System.out.println("Car is driving");
    }
}
```

In this case, Car is a type of Drivable. The Car class provides its own implementation of the drive method, but the way it drives is not dictated by the Drivable interface.

This approach provides a high level of abstraction and allows for loose coupling between classes, which makes your code more flexible and easier to maintain and test.

Remember, while interfaces are powerful, they should be used judiciously. Overusing interfaces can lead to unnecessary complexity. Always consider the specific needs of your project when deciding whether to use interfaces.

◦ **Favoring Static Member Classes Over Nonstatic in Java**

In Java, nested classes are divided into two categories: static and non-static. Non-static nested classes are known as inner classes. A static nested class is behaviorally a top-level class that has been nested in another top-level class for packaging convenience.

Static vs Non-Static

A key difference between static and non-static nested classes is that a non-static nested class has access to the instance variables and methods of the outer class. A static nested class does not have a reference to a nesting instance, so it can't access the instance variables without an explicit outer class object.

```java
public class OuterClass {
  private int x = 10;

  class InnerClass {
    public void printX() {
      System.out.println(x);  // Can access outer class's instance variable
    }
  }

  static class StaticNestedClass {
    public void printX(OuterClass oc) {
      System.out.println(oc.x);  // Needs an object of outer class to access 'x'
    }
  }
}
```

Why Favor Static Member Classes Over Nonstatic?

There are several reasons to favor static member classes over non-static ones:

1. Encapsulation

Non-static nested classes have a hidden reference to the instance of the outer class. This could lead to a memory leak if the instance of the inner class lives longer than the instance of the outer class. Static nested classes do not have this problem.

2. Readability and Maintainability

Static member classes make your code more readable and maintainable. Since they don't depend on the instance of the outer class, it is clearer that they can be used independently.

3. Performance

Non-static nested classes use more memory due to the extra reference to the outer class instance. If you don't need this reference, using a static nested class is more efficient.

When to Use Non-Static Nested Classes?

Despite the advantages of static nested classes, there are scenarios where non-static nested classes are useful. For example, if behavior is tightly coupled with the state of an outer instance, using a non-static nested class makes sense.

While both static and non-static nested classes have their uses, static nested classes are generally preferable. They promote encapsulation and make your code more readable and maintainable. Non-static nested classes, or inner classes, should only be used when there is a compelling reason to allow the nested class to access the non-public elements of the outer class. As with many aspects of programming, the choice between static and non-static depends on the specific needs of your project.

○ Limiting source files to a single top-level class

Readability

When a file contains only one top-level class, it's easier to understand the structure and behavior of that class without the distraction of other classes.

Maintainability

It's easier to maintain and update code when classes are organized in this way. Changes to one class don't have to consider the impact on a second class in the same file.

Avoiding Naming Conflicts

Java requires that the file name match the name of the public class it contains. If you have more than one top-level class in a file, you can't make them all public, leading to potential visibility issues.

Compilation

The Java compiler creates a separate bytecode file (.class file) for each top-level class. Keeping each top-level class in a separate source file can make the compilation process more straightforward and help avoid any confusion about where to find the bytecode for a class.

Here's an example of how you might organize your classes:

```
// File: Bird.java
public class Bird {
    // Class definition
}

// File: Mammal.java
public class Mammal {
    // Class definition
}
```

In this example, each class is defined in its own file, making the code easier to read, maintain, and compile.

Using raw types in Java is generally not recommended.

Type Safety

Generics provide stronger type checks at compile time. A Java collection using generics has compile time safety because it holds a specific type of elements so it cannot hold any other type of elements, thus eliminating the risk of ClassCastException that was common while working with collection classes.

Here's an example of using raw types:

```
List list = new ArrayList();
list.add("hello");
list.add(1); // This compiles fine, but could cause problems later
```

In this example, the list can hold any type of object, so there's no way to ensure at compile time that we're not adding an inappropriate object to the list.

Now, let's see how this code could be written using generics:

```
List<String> list = new ArrayList<>();
list.add("hello");
list.add(1); // This line would cause a compile error
```

In this example, the list is explicitly restricted to hold only strings. Trying to add an integer to the list results in a compile error, preventing potential problems at runtime.

Clarity

Using generics makes your code easier to read and understand. Without generics, you have to cast every object you read from your collection. With generics, it's clear what type of objects are stored in the collection.

Remember, while raw types are still supported in Java for compatibility reasons, their use is strongly discouraged in new code.

○ **Type-safe heterogeneous containers**

Are a powerful concept in Java. They allow you to create a single container that can hold objects of any type, while still maintaining type safety.

Here's an example of how you might create a type-safe heterogeneous container using a Map:

```java
public class HeterogeneousContainer {
  private Map<Class<?>, Object> elements = new HashMap<>();

  public <T> void putElement(Class<T> type, T instance) {
    if (type == null) {
      throw new NullPointerException("Type is null");
    }
    elements.put(type, instance);
  }

  public <T> T getElement(Class<T> type) {
    return type.cast(elements.get(type));
  }
}
```

In this example, HeterogeneousContainer can hold any type of object, and you can retrieve elements from the container with their correct types:

```java
HeterogeneousContainer container = new HeterogeneousContainer();
container.putElement(String.class, "Hello");
container.putElement(Integer.class, 123);

String s = container.getElement(String.class);
Integer n = container.getElement(Integer.class);
```

This approach provides type safety because you can't accidentally insert an object of the wrong type into the container, and when you retrieve an element, you get an object of the correct type.

Remember, while type-safe heterogeneous containers are powerful, they should be used judiciously. Overusing them can lead to unnecessarily complex code. Always consider the specific needs of your project when deciding whether to use them.

○ **Eliminating Unchecked Warnings in Java**

Introduction

Unchecked warnings are issued by the Java compiler when it encounters code that is not type-safe, but the code could potentially execute without errors. It's a warning, not an error, because the Java language supports these constructs for backward compatibility.

Understanding Unchecked Warnings

Unchecked warnings typically occur when using legacy code where generics are not used. Here's an example:

```
List myList = new ArrayList();
myList.add("Hello");
String s = (String) myList.get(0); // Unchecked warning here
```

In this example, the compiler issues an unchecked warning because it can't guarantee that the object retrieved from the list is a String.

Using Generics to Eliminate Unchecked Warnings

Generics provide a way for you to communicate the type of a collection to the compiler, so it can be checked. Once the compiler knows the type of object the collection is supposed to hold, it can check to make sure you have treated the collection consistently. Here's how you can fix the above example:

```
List<String> myList = new ArrayList<>();
myList.add("Hello");
String s = myList.get(0); // No unchecked warning
```

Now, the compiler knows that myList is supposed to hold strings, so it can ensure that you don't try to put an Integer or some other class into myList.

Suppressing Unchecked Warnings

If you can't fix the unchecked warning, as may be the case if you're interfacing with non-generic legacy code, you can suppress the warning using the @SuppressWarnings("unchecked") annotation:

```
@SuppressWarnings("unchecked")
public void myMethod() {
   // Method code here
}
```

But use this sparingly, and only when you're sure that the code won't cause problems at runtime. It's usually better to fix the problem than to suppress the warning.

Unchecked warnings are important because they point out areas in your code where you might have a ClassCastException at runtime. The Java Generics mechanism is there to help catch these errors at compile time. Using generics, especially when dealing with collections, can help eliminate these unchecked warnings and make your code safer and more robust.

○ Preferring Lists to Arrays in Java

In Java, both lists (List) and arrays are used to store data. However, lists are generally preferred over arrays for several reasons.

Flexibility

Lists in Java are more flexible than arrays. They can grow and shrink dynamically, while the size of an array is fixed at the time of creation.

```
List<String> list = new ArrayList<>();
list.add("Hello"); // You can add elements as needed

String[] array = new String[10];
array[0] = "Hello"; // The size of the array is fixed
```

High-Level Operations

Lists in Java come with high-level operations that make it easy to manipulate the data. For example, you can easily add, remove, or replace elements in a list. Arrays do not have these built-in methods, so you often have to write more code to perform these operations.

Type Safety

Lists in Java are integrated with Java's type system, ensuring type safety. When you use a list, you specify the type of elements it can contain. This is not the case with arrays, which can lead to runtime errors.

While arrays are a fundamental part of many programming languages, lists in Java offer several advantages that make them a better choice in many situations. They are more flexible, easier to work with, and provide stronger type safety. So, when in doubt, prefer lists to arrays.

for the confusion. Here's the article in English:

○ **Favoring generic types is a key principle in Java**

Type Safety

Generics provide compile-time type safety, ensuring that you don't insert an object of the wrong type into a collection. This helps prevent ClassCastException at runtime.

```
List<String> list = new ArrayList<>();
list.add("Hello"); // OK
list.add(123); // Compile error
```

Code Reusability

Generics enable you to write a method or class that can work with any type of object, while still maintaining type safety.

```
public static <T> void printArray(T[] array) {
   for (T element : array) {
      System.out.println(element);
   }
}
```

In this example, printArray can work with an array of any type.

Eliminating Type Casting

Without generics, you have to cast every object you read from a collection. With generics, it's clear what type of objects are stored in the collection, eliminating the need for casting.

```
List list = new ArrayList();
list.add("Hello");
String s = (String) list.get(0); // Requires casting

List<String> genericList = new ArrayList<>();
genericList.add("Hello");
String str = genericList.get(0); // No casting required
```

Remember, while generics are powerful, they should be used judiciously. Overusing generics can lead to unnecessarily complex code. Always consider the specific needs of your project when deciding whether to use generics.

◦ Favoring Generic Methods in Java

Generic methods are methods that introduce their own type parameters. This is similar to declaring a generic type, but the type parameter's scope is limited to the method where it's declared. Static and non-static methods, as well as constructors, can be generic.

Why Favor Generic Methods?

1. Stronger Type Checks at Compile Time

A Java compiler applies strong type checking to generic code and issues errors if the code violates type safety. Fixing compile-time errors is easier than fixing runtime errors, which can be difficult to find.

2. Elimination of Casts

The following code snippet without generics requires casting:

```
List list = new ArrayList();
list.add("Hello World");
String s = (String) list.get(0);
```

When re-written to use generics, the code does not require casting:

```
List<String> list = new ArrayList<>();
list.add("Hello World");
String s = list.get(0);
```

3. Enabling Programmers to Implement Generic Algorithms

By using generics, programmers can implement generic algorithms that work on collections of different types, can be customized, and are type-safe and easier to read.

Generic Method Examples

Generic methods are methods that introduce their own type parameters. Here is an example:

```
public static <T> void fromArrayToCollection(T[] a, Collection<T> c) {
    for (T o : a) {
        c.add(o); // Correct
    }
}
```

In this example, T is the type parameter that represents the type of elements in the array and the collection.

Using generics, especially in methods, can make your Java code type-safe, more readable, and more robust. When you design your methods, you should consider whether they could be made generic.

Bounded wildcards are a powerful feature in Java generics that can greatly increase the flexibility of your API. Here's why:

- ○ **Understanding Bounded Wildcards**

Bounded wildcards are used to restrict the unknown type (?) to a certain range of types. There are two types of bounded wildcards:

- Upper Bounded Wildcards (<? extends T>): These are used when you want to relax the restrictions on a variable. You can use an upper bounded wildcard when you want to access the objects in a data structure using methods in the class specified by the upper bound.

- Lower Bounded Wildcards (<? super T>): These are used when you need to put objects in a data structure and access the data structure using methods in the class specified by the lower bound.

Increasing API Flexibility

Bounded wildcards can increase the flexibility of your API by allowing a greater range of inputs. For example, consider a method that operates on lists of Number objects:

```
public void process(List<Number> list) {
    // Method body
}
```

This method can only accept a List of Number objects. It cannot accept a List of Integer or a List of Double, even though Integer and Double are subclasses of Number.

By using an upper bounded wildcard, you can make this method more flexible:

```
public void process(List<? extends Number> list) {
    // Method body
}
```

Now, the method can accept a List of any subclass of Number, increasing its flexibility.

Remember, while bounded wildcards can make your API more flexible, they can also make your code more complex. It's important to use them judiciously and only when necessary.

Combining generics and varargs in Java needs to be done judiciously because it can lead to confusing errors and unexpected behavior. Here's why:

- ○ **Type Erasure and Heap Pollution**

Generics in Java uses type erasure, which means the generic type information is not available at runtime. Varargs methods are implemented as an array, and arrays in Java have a runtime type that must be known. When you combine generics and varargs, you can end up with a situation called heap pollution.

Heap pollution occurs when a variable of a parameterized type refers to an object that is not of that parameterized type. This can happen when calling a varargs method with a non-reifiable varargs type. Non-reifiable types are those whose runtime representation has less information than their compile-time representation.

Here's an example of a method that causes a heap pollution warning:

```java
@SafeVarargs
public static <T> List<T> asList(T... elements) {
    List<T> list = new ArrayList<>();
    for (T element : elements) {
        list.add(element);
    }
    return list;
}
```

In this example, the asList method is a generic varargs method that can cause heap pollution. If you call this method with arguments of different types, the array created to hold the varargs parameter will have a runtime type of the most specific type common to all arguments, which can lead to a ClassCastException at runtime.

Using @SafeVarargs Annotation

The @SafeVarargs annotation is a mechanism included in Java 7 and later that suppresses heap pollution warnings related to the use of varargs methods with generic arguments. You should only use this annotation when you are sure that the implementation of the method will not result in heap pollution.

Remember, while combining generics and varargs can provide powerful functionality, it should be done carefully and judiciously to avoid runtime errors and ensure type safety.

○ **Enums or int constants**

Certainly! Let's delve into the benefits of using **enums** over **int constants** in Java. Enums provide a more robust and expressive way to represent a fixed set of related values. Here are some compelling reasons to favor enums:

1. **Type Safety and Readability**:

   - Enums allow you to define a specific set of named constants with a clear type. This ensures type safety during compilation.
   - Compare this to using int constants or String variables, where you might accidentally assign an incorrect value or misspell a constant name.

2. **Limited Set of Values**:

   - Enums restrict the possible values to a predefined set. This prevents accidental misuse or invalid inputs.
   - For example, consider player types like "ARCHER," "WARRIOR," and "SORCERER." Using enums, you can define:

   ```
   enum PlayerType {
       ARCHER,
       WARRIOR,
       SORCERER
   }
   ```

3. **Compile-Time Checks**:

   - When you use enums, the compiler ensures that you only use valid enum values. If you try to assign an incompatible value, it results in a compile-time error.
   - For instance:

   ```
   PlayerType playerType = PlayerType.MALE; // Compile-time error
   ```

4. **Additional Information and Behavior**:

   - Enums can carry additional information (such as labels, descriptions, or associated values) beyond their names.
   - You can also add methods to enums, making them more versatile.
   - Example:

   ```
   enum Gender {
       MALE("Male"),
       FEMALE("Female");

       private final String label;

       Gender(String label) {
   ```

76

```
      this.label = label;
   }

   public String getLabel() {
      return label;
   }
}
```

5. **Improved Code Readability**:

   - Enum constants have self-explanatory names, enhancing code readability.
   - Compare:

     String gender = Constants.MALE; // Less clear

     vs.

     Gender gender = Gender.MALE; // Clearly indicates the intent

6. **Serialization and JSON Conversion**:

   - Enums serialize naturally to their names, making them suitable for APIs and persistence.
   - When converting objects to JSON (e.g., for web services), enums are more straightforward:

     ```
     // Using enums
     PlayerType playerType = PlayerType.ARCHER;
     String json = toJson(playerType); // Converts to "ARCHER"

     // Using constants
     String playerType = Constants.ARCHER;
     // Manually map to JSON: {"playerType": "ARCHER"}
     ```

In summary, enums provide better type safety, readability, and maintainability. They are especially useful when you need a fixed set of related values with associated behavior. So, next time you encounter a scenario like this, consider using enums for a cleaner and safer codebase!

○ In Java: Use Instance Fields Instead of Ordinals

When working with enums in Java, it's essential to choose the right approach for representing related values. In this article, we'll explore why using **instance fields** in enums is preferable over relying on **ordinals**.

1. The Basics: Enums and Ordinals

First, let's recap what enums and ordinals are:

- **Enums**: An enum is a special data type that represents a fixed set of named constants. Each constant is an instance of the enum type.
- **Ordinals**: The ordinal value of an enum constant is its position within the enum declaration (starting from zero).

2. The Pitfall of Ordinals

While ordinals seem convenient, they come with limitations:

- **Brittleness**: Ordinals are fragile because any change in the enum's order (adding, removing, or rearranging constants) affects their values. This can break existing code.
- **Semantic Ambiguity**: Ordinals lack semantic meaning. For example, consider an enum representing days of the week:

```
enum DayOfWeek {
    MONDAY, TUESDAY, WEDNESDAY, THURSDAY, FRIDAY, SATURDAY, SUNDAY
}
```

The ordinal for TUESDAY is 1, but what does that tell us about Tuesday itself?

3. Why Use Instance Fields?

By using instance fields, we address the shortcomings of ordinals:

- **Explicit Values**: Assign meaningful values to each enum constant using instance fields. For example:

```
enum DayOfWeek {
    MONDAY(1), TUESDAY(2), WEDNESDAY(3), THURSDAY(4), FRIDAY(5),
SATURDAY(6), SUNDAY(7);

    private final int dayNumber;

    DayOfWeek(int dayNumber) {
        this.dayNumber = dayNumber;
```

```
    }

    public int getDayNumber() {
        return dayNumber;
    }
}
```

Now we can access the day number directly: DayOfWeek.TUESDAY.getDayNumber() returns 2.

- **Robustness**: Instance fields are resilient to changes in enum order. Adding or reordering constants won't affect their assigned values.

4. Best Practices

When using enums, follow these best practices:

- **Avoid Reliance on Ordinals**: Refrain from using ordinal() unless absolutely necessary (e.g., for legacy compatibility).
- **Use Instance Fields**: Whenever possible, define instance fields to store additional information related to each enum constant.
- **Document Your Enums**: Provide clear documentation for the purpose and usage of each enum constant.

In Java, favor instance fields over ordinals for enums. By doing so, you create more robust, expressive, and maintainable code. Enums with meaningful values enhance readability and reduce the risk of subtle bugs. So, next time you define an enum, consider using instance fields—it's a cleaner and safer approach!

○ EnumSet vs. Bit Fields in Java

1. The Basics

- **Bit Fields**: Bit fields (also known as bit flags) are an efficient way to store multiple related boolean values within a single primitive type. Typically, an integer (e.g., int) is used to represent these flags, with each bit corresponding to a specific flag.
- **EnumSet**: EnumSet is a specialized collection class in Java designed specifically for working with enum constants. It provides the efficiency of bit flags while maintaining type safety and readability.

2. The Pitfalls of Bit Fields

a. Lack of Type Safety

- Bit fields are not type-safe. You're essentially manipulating raw bits, which can lead to errors and bugs.
- For example, consider the following bit field:

```
int permissions = 0;
permissions |= READ_PERMISSION;
permissions |= WRITE_PERMISSION;
```

b. Brittleness

- Bit fields are fragile. If you change the order or add/remove flags, existing code may break.
- Debugging issues related to bit manipulation can be challenging.

3. Why Use EnumSet?

a. Type Safety

- EnumSet operates on enum constants, ensuring type safety. You work with meaningful names rather than raw integers.
- Example:

```
enum Permission {
   READ, WRITE, EXECUTE
}

EnumSet<Permission> permissions = EnumSet.of(Permission.READ, Permission.WRITE);
```

b. Efficiency

- Internally, EnumSet uses bit vectors (similar to bit fields), making it efficient in terms of memory and performance.
- EnumSet is optimized for enum constants and performs well even with large sets.

c. Readable Code

- EnumSet code is more expressive and self-documenting:

```
if (permissions.contains(Permission.WRITE)) {
    // Handle write permission
}
```

d. Serialization and Persistence

- EnumSet can be easily serialized (e.g., to a database) without manual bit manipulation.
- You can store the entire set of enum constants directly.

4. Best Practices

- **Prefer EnumSet**: Whenever you need to manage a set of related enum constants, use EnumSet.
- **Avoid Raw Bit Manipulation**: Reserve bit fields for low-level scenarios where performance is critical and type safety can be sacrificed.

In modern Java, EnumSet strikes a balance between efficiency and safety. By using EnumSet, you get the benefits of bit fields without compromising type safety. So, next time you encounter a situation involving flags or permissions, consider reaching for EnumSet—it's a cleaner and safer choice!

○ **Use EnumMap Instead of Ordinal Indexing in Java**

When working with enums in Java, it's essential to choose the right data structure for efficient and type-safe handling of enum constants. In this article, we'll explore why using EnumMap is a better alternative to ordinal indexing.

1. The Basics: Enums and Ordinals

First, let's recap what enums and ordinals are:

- **Enums**: An enum is a special data type that represents a fixed set of named constants. Each constant is an instance of the enum type.
- **Ordinals**: The ordinal value of an enum constant is its position within the enum declaration (starting from zero).

2. The Pitfalls of Ordinal Indexing

a. Lack of Type Safety

- Ordinals are not type-safe. When using ordinal() to index an array or perform other operations, you're essentially working with raw integers.
- This lack of type safety can lead to errors and bugs.

b. Brittleness

- Ordinals are fragile. If you change the order of enum constants (e.g., add, remove, or rearrange them), existing code relying on ordinals may break.
- Debugging issues related to ordinal manipulation can be challenging.

3. Why Use EnumMap?

a. Type Safety and Readability

- EnumMap operates on enum constants, ensuring type safety. You work with meaningful names rather than raw integers.
- Example:

```
enum DayOfWeek {
    MONDAY, TUESDAY, WEDNESDAY, THURSDAY, FRIDAY, SATURDAY,
SUNDAY
}

EnumMap<DayOfWeek, String> tasks = new
EnumMap<>(DayOfWeek.class);
tasks.put(DayOfWeek.MONDAY, "Write code");
```

b. Efficiency

- Internally, EnumMap uses an array (similar to ordinal indexing), but it hides this implementation detail.
- It's optimized for enum constants and performs well even with large sets.

c. Readable Code

- EnumMap code is expressive and self-documenting:

```
if (tasks.containsKey(DayOfWeek.TUESDAY)) {
    // Handle Tuesday's task
}
```

d. Serialization and Persistence

- EnumMap can be easily serialized (e.g., to a database) without manual bit manipulation.
- You can store the entire set of enum constants directly.

4. Best Practices

- **Prefer EnumMap**: Whenever you need to associate values with enum constants, use EnumMap.
- **Avoid Raw Ordinal Indexing**: Reserve ordinal indexing for low-level scenarios where performance is critical and type safety can be sacrificed.

In modern Java, EnumMap strikes a balance between efficiency and safety. By using EnumMap, you get the benefits of ordinal indexing without compromising type safety. So, next time you work with enum constants, consider reaching for EnumMap—it's a cleaner and safer choice!

- **Emulating Extensible Enums with Interfaces in Java**

Enums in Java provide a powerful way to define a fixed set of named constants. However, they have limitations when it comes to extensibility. While you cannot directly extend an enum type, you can achieve similar functionality by using interfaces alongside enums. Let's explore how to emulate extensible enums using interfaces.

1. The Challenge: Extending Enums

Consider a basic enum representing string operations:

```
public enum BasicStringOperation {
    TRIM("Removing leading and trailing spaces."),
    TO_UPPER("Changing all characters into upper case."),
    REVERSE("Reversing the given string.");

    private final String description;

    BasicStringOperation(String description) {
        this.description = description;
    }

    public String getDescription() {
        return description;
    }
}
```

Now imagine we want to add new string operations (e.g., MD5 encoding or BASE64 encoding) to this enum. Unfortunately, directly extending enums is not allowed in Java.

2. The Solution: Using Interfaces

To overcome this limitation, we can create an interface that accompanies our basic enum. The enum will then implement this interface, allowing clients to create their own enums that also implement the same interface.

Example:

```
// Define an interface for extensible string operations
interface StringOperation {
    String getDescription();
}

// BasicStringOperation enum implements the StringOperation interface
public enum BasicStringOperation implements StringOperation {
    TRIM("Removing leading and trailing spaces."),
    TO_UPPER("Changing all characters into upper case."),
    REVERSE("Reversing the given string.");
```

```java
  private final String description;

  BasicStringOperation(String description) {
     this.description = description;
  }

  @Override
  public String getDescription() {
     return description;
  }
}

// Client-specific enum implementing StringOperation
enum ExtendedStringOperation implements StringOperation {
   MD5_ENCODE("Encoding the given string using the MD5 algorithm."),
   BASE64_ENCODE("Encoding the given string using the BASE64 algorithm.");

   private final String description;

   ExtendedStringOperation(String description) {
      this.description = description;
   }

   @Override
   public String getDescription() {
      return description;
   }
}
```

3. Benefits of Emulating Extensible Enums

- **Type Safety**: By using interfaces, we maintain type safety while allowing extensibility.
- **Readable Code**: Enums implementing the interface provide self-documenting code.
- **Serialization and Persistence**: Enums can be easily serialized without manual bit manipulation.

While true extensible enums are not directly supported, emulating them with interfaces provides a clean and effective solution. So, next time you need extensibility in your enums, consider this approach —it's a strategic way to enhance your code!

- **Annotations vs. Naming Patterns in Java**

   ### 1. The Basics

- **Annotations**: Annotations are metadata added to Java code elements (such as classes, methods, fields, or parameters). They provide additional information that can be processed at compile time or runtime.
- **Naming Patterns**: Naming conventions involve following specific naming rules for variables, methods, classes, etc., to improve code readability and maintainability.

2. Advantages of Annotations

a. Structured Metadata

- Annotations allow you to attach structured metadata to code elements. This metadata can be used by tools, frameworks, or custom processors.
- Example:

```
@Entity
public class Product {
    // ...
}
```

b. Reduced Boilerplate Code

- Annotations reduce boilerplate code by automating repetitive tasks.
- For instance, frameworks like Spring use annotations to configure dependency injection, eliminating the need for XML configuration files.

c. Compile-Time Checks

- Annotations enable compile-time checks. For example, @Override ensures that a method overrides a superclass method.
- Detecting errors early during compilation improves code quality.

d. Customization and Configuration

- Annotations allow developers to customize behavior without modifying the core code.

- You can create your own annotations to define custom behavior (e.g., for logging, security, or validation).

3. Common Annotations

a. @Override

- Ensures that a method overrides a superclass method.
- Helps catch accidental method signature changes.

b. @Deprecated

- Marks a method, class, or field as deprecated.
- Provides a warning to developers when using deprecated elements.

c. @Entity

- Used in JPA (Java Persistence API) to mark a class as an entity.
- Enables automatic database table generation.

4. When to Use Naming Patterns

- Naming patterns are still valuable for consistency and readability.
- Use them for naming conventions like camelCase, PascalCase, or ALL_CAPS.

Annotations enhance code expressiveness, reduce boilerplate, and enable powerful features. While naming patterns remain essential, annotations provide a more structured and dynamic way to enrich your Java code. So, next time you need to convey metadata or automate tasks, consider reaching for annotations—it's a cleaner and more extensible approach!

- **Marker Interfaces in Java**

In Java, a **marker interface** (also known as a **tagging interface**) is an interface that doesn't contain any methods or constants. Instead, it serves as a way to provide additional information about objects at runtime. Marker interfaces act as indicators to the compiler and JVM, influencing their behavior.

1. JDK Built-In Marker Interfaces

Java includes several built-in marker interfaces, each serving a specific purpose:

1. **Serializable**:

   - Objects implementing this interface can be serialized (converted to a byte stream) and deserialized.
   - When using ObjectOutputStream.writeObject(), the JVM checks if the object implements Serializable. If not, a NotSerializableException is thrown.

2. **Cloneable**:

   - Indicates that an object can be cloned using the Object.clone() method.
   - If an object doesn't implement Cloneable, attempting to clone it results in a CloneNotSupportedException.

3. **Remote**:

   - Used in distributed computing and remote method invocation (RMI).
   - Objects implementing Remote can be accessed remotely across different JVMs.

2. Custom Marker Interfaces

You can create your own marker interfaces tailored to your application's needs. Let's create a simple example:

Suppose we want to indicate whether an object can be removed from a database. We'll define a custom marker interface called Deletable:

```
public interface Deletable { }

public class Entity implements Deletable {
  // Implementation details for Entity
}

public class ShapeDao {
  // Other DAO methods

  public boolean delete(Object object) {
    if (!(object instanceof Deletable)) {
      return false; // Cannot delete non-Deletable objects
    }
```

```
    // Delete implementation details
    return true;
  }
}
```

In the ShapeDao class, the delete() method ensures that only objects implementing Deletable can be deleted from the database. This way, we give an indication to the JVM about the runtime behavior of our objects.

3. Marker Interfaces vs. Annotations

While marker interfaces are still in use, newer development often favors **annotations** to achieve similar goals. Here's the key difference:

- **Marker Interfaces**:
    - Provide runtime information.
    - Blur the lines of what an interface represents (since they don't define behavior).
    - Allow polymorphism.
- **Annotations**:
    - Attach metadata to code elements.
    - Can be applied to classes, methods, fields, etc.
    - Offer more flexibility and customization.

In summary, marker interfaces serve as a historical approach, while annotations provide a more versatile and expressive way to convey metadata. Choose wisely based on your specific requirements!

○ **The @Override Annotation**

The @Override annotation is a powerful tool that serves two primary purposes:

1. **Compile-Time Checking**:

   - When you use @Override, the compiler ensures that the method you're annotating actually overrides a method from a superclass or implements an interface method.
   - If there's a mismatch (e.g., misspelled method name or incorrect parameters), the compiler will issue a warning or error.
   - This helps catch subtle bugs early during compilation.

2. **Code Clarity and Intent**:

   - By explicitly marking overridden methods with @Override, you make your code more readable and self-documenting.
   - It indicates to other developers (and your future self) that this method intentionally overrides a parent method or implements an interface method.
   - When reading the code, it's immediately clear that the method has a specific purpose related to the superclass or interface.

Example Usage

Consider the following scenario:

```
class Animal {
  void makeSound() {
    System.out.println("Animal makes a sound");
  }
}

class Dog extends Animal {
  @Override
  void makeSound() {
    System.out.println("Dog barks");
  }
}
```

In this example:

- The Dog class overrides the makeSound() method from its superclass Animal.
- Without @Override, it would still compile, but you'd lose the compile-time check and the explicit indication of intent.

Best Practices

1. **Always Use @Override**:

   - Make it a habit to annotate every method that you intend to override.
   - Even if it seems redundant, consistency is crucial for maintaining code quality.

2. **Interface Methods**:

   - In Java 6 and later, you can also use @Override for methods that implement an interface.
   - This provides similar benefits: compile-time checking and clarity.

3. **IDE Support**:

   - Most modern IDEs highlight overridden methods when you use @Override.
   - Some IDEs even automatically add the annotation when you override a method.

In summary, consistently using @Override is a good practice. It helps prevent mistakes, improves code readability, and ensures that your intentions align with the superclass or interface. So, keep annotating those overridden methods!

○ **Lambda Expressions vs. Anonymous Inner Classes**

Both lambda expressions and anonymous inner classes allow you to define behavior for functional interfaces (interfaces with a single unimplemented method). However, they have distinct characteristics:

1. **Syntax**:

   - **Lambda Expressions**: A lambda expression is essentially a concise method definition without a name. It uses the -> syntax.
   - **Anonymous Inner Classes**: An anonymous inner class provides a class definition and instantiates it at the same time. It uses the new keyword and the name of the class or interface being implemented.

2. **Type Safety**:

   - **Lambda Expressions**: Lambdas are type-safe. The compiler ensures that the lambda expression matches the functional interface's method signature.
   - **Anonymous Inner Classes**: While anonymous inner classes also provide type safety, lambdas are more concise and expressive.

3. **Readability**:

   - **Lambda Expressions**: Lambdas make code more readable by eliminating boilerplate. They focus on the behavior rather than the class structure.
   - **Anonymous Inner Classes**: Anonymous classes can be verbose, especially for simple tasks. They require additional syntax for class definition.

4. **Performance**:

   - **Lambda Expressions**: Lambdas use the invokedynamic instruction (introduced in JDK 7), which is generally efficient. They don't create additional class files during compilation.

Using Lambda Expression:

```
public class LambdaExample {
  public static void main(String[] args) {
    Runnable task = () -> System.out.println("Task executed using lambda");
    new Thread(task).start();
  }
}
```

Using Anonymous Inner Class:

```
public class AnonymousClassExample {
    public static void main(String[] args) {
        Runnable task = new Runnable() {
            @Override
            public void run() {
                System.out.println("Task executed using anonymous inner class");
            }
        };
        new Thread(task).start();
    }
}
```

In both cases, we achieve the same result: executing a task in a separate thread. However, the lambda version is more concise and expressive.

While both approaches have their place, lambdas are preferred for their readability, conciseness, and type safety. So, next time you need to implement a functional interface, consider reaching for a lambda —it's a cleaner and more modern choice!

○ **Method References vs. Lambdas**

Both method references and lambdas allow you to express behavior concisely, especially when working with functional interfaces. However, method references offer some advantages:

1. **Readability**:

   - **Method References**: They provide a clear and direct link to an existing method. The syntax is minimal, making the code more readable.
   - **Lambdas**: While lambdas are concise, they can become less readable for complex expressions.

2. **Reuse of Existing Methods**:

   - **Method References**: You can reuse methods from existing classes or instances. This promotes code reuse and adheres to the DRY (Don't Repeat Yourself) principle.
   - **Lambdas**: Lambdas are more suitable for inline expressions or short-lived behavior.

3. **Types of Method References**:

   - **Static Method References**: Refers to a static method (e.g., Math::sqrt).
   - **Instance Method References**: Refers to an instance method of a specific object (e.g., String::length).
   - **Constructor References**: Refers to a constructor (e.g., ArrayList::new).

Examples

Using Method Reference:

```
import java.util.List;
import java.util.stream.Collectors;

public class MethodReferenceExample {
    public static void main(String[] args) {
        List<String> words = List.of("apple", "banana", "cherry");

        // Using method reference to String::toUpperCase
        List<String> uppercaseWords = words.stream()
            .map(String::toUpperCase)
            .collect(Collectors.toList());

        System.out.println(uppercaseWords);
    }
}
```

Using Lambda:

```java
import java.util.List;
import java.util.stream.Collectors;

public class LambdaExample {
    public static void main(String[] args) {
        List<String> words = List.of("apple", "banana", "cherry");

        // Using lambda expression
        List<String> uppercaseWords = words.stream()
            .map(word -> word.toUpperCase())
            .collect(Collectors.toList());

        System.out.println(uppercaseWords);
    }
}
```

In both cases, we transform a list of words to uppercase. The method reference version (String::toUpperCase) is more concise and directly conveys the intent.

While both method references and lambdas have their place, method references shine when you want to reuse existing methods and keep your code clean. So, next time you need to express behavior, consider reaching for a method reference—it's a cleaner and more expressive choice!

- **Standard Functional Interfaces**

In Java, standard functional interfaces are predefined interfaces that represent common functional patterns. They are part of the java.util.function package and provide a consistent way to work with lambdas and method references. Using these interfaces promotes code readability, reusability, and adherence to functional programming principles.

Here are some commonly used standard functional interfaces:

1. **Function<T, R>:**

   - Represents a function that takes an argument of type T and produces a result of type R.
   - Example: Mapping a list of strings to their lengths.

2. **Predicate<T>:**

   - Represents a boolean-valued function that takes an argument of type T.
   - Useful for filtering or testing conditions.
   - Example: Checking if a number is even.

3. **Consumer<T>:**

   - Represents an operation that takes an argument of type T and performs some action (but doesn't return a result).
   - Example: Printing elements of a list.

4. **Supplier<T>:**

   - Represents a supplier of results (no input arguments).
   - Useful for lazy initialization or generating values.
   - Example: Creating random numbers.

5. **BiFunction<T, U, R>:**

   - Represents a function that takes two arguments of types T and U, and produces a result of type R.
   - Example: Combining two lists into a map.

Benefits of Using Standard Functional Interfaces

1. **Consistency**:

   - Standard functional interfaces follow a consistent naming convention (Function, Predicate, etc.), making them easy to recognize.
   - Developers familiar with these interfaces can quickly understand their purpose.

2. **Interoperability**:

   - Standard interfaces can be used seamlessly with other Java APIs and libraries.
   - For example, they integrate well with streams, optionals, and CompletableFuture.

3. **Avoid Reinventing the Wheel**:

- Instead of creating custom functional interfaces, leverage the existing standard ones.
- This reduces boilerplate code and encourages best practices.

Example Usage

```java
import java.util.List;
import java.util.function.Function;
import java.util.function.Predicate;

public class StandardFunctionalInterfacesExample {
  public static void main(String[] args) {
    List<String> words = List.of("apple", "banana", "cherry");

    // Example 1: Function to get word lengths
    Function<String, Integer> wordLengthFunction = String::length;
    words.forEach(word -> System.out.println("Length of " + word + ": " + wordLengthFunction.apply(word)));

    // Example 2: Predicate to filter words starting with 'b'
    Predicate<String> startsWithB = word -> word.startsWith("b");
    words.stream()
        .filter(startsWithB)
        .forEach(System.out::println);
  }
}
```

In this example, we use the Function and Predicate interfaces to calculate word lengths and filter words starting with 'b', respectively.

Standard functional interfaces simplify functional programming in Java. By using them consistently, you enhance code readability and adhere to established patterns. So, next time you work with lambdas, consider reaching for these standard interfaces—it's a cleaner and more efficient approach!

1. **Prefer Streams for Collection Processing**:

   - Streams are particularly useful for processing collections of data, such as lists or arrays.
   - They provide a concise and declarative syntax for transforming, filtering, and aggregating data.
   - When you need to perform operations on a collection, consider using streams instead of traditional loop constructs.

2. **Use Intermediate and Terminal Operations Wisely**:

   - Streams consist of intermediate and terminal operations.
   - Intermediate operations transform the data in the stream, while terminal operations produce a result or a side effect.
   - It's important to use these operations wisely and avoid unnecessary operations.

3. **Lazy Evaluation and Short-Circuiting**:

   - Streams support lazy evaluation, meaning that intermediate operations are not executed until a terminal operation is invoked.
   - This allows for efficient processing by avoiding unnecessary computations.
   - Additionally, streams support short-circuiting, where processing stops as soon as the desired result is obtained. Utilize these features to optimize performance and reduce unnecessary computations.

4. **Consider Parallel Streams for Large Datasets**:

   - Parallel streams allow for concurrent execution of operations on large datasets, potentially improving performance on multi-core systems.
   - However, parallelism introduces additional overhead and is most effective when applied to computationally intensive tasks.
   - Evaluate the characteristics of your data and the nature of the operations to determine if parallel streams are appropriate.

5. **Don't Overuse Streams for Simple Tasks**:

   - While streams provide powerful capabilities, they are not always the best choice for every situation.
   - For simple tasks that involve iterating over a small collection or performing basic operations, traditional loop constructs (such as for or foreach loops) may be more readable and straightforward.
   - Use streams when they offer clear advantages in terms of expressiveness and readability.

6. **Consider Compatibility and Backward Compatibility**:

   - Be mindful of the Java version you are targeting when using streams.
   - Some stream features and methods were introduced in later versions of Java.

- If you need to maintain backward compatibility with older Java versions, ensure that your code is compatible and provide appropriate fallback solutions if needed.

Remember that while streams provide powerful abstractions, thoughtful usage ensures that your code remains maintainable and efficient.

Side-Effect-Free Functions in Streams

1. **What Are Side Effects?**

   - A **side effect** occurs when a function modifies state outside its scope (e.g., changing global variables, modifying objects, or printing to the console).
   - In functional programming, side effects are discouraged because they can lead to unexpected behavior and make code harder to reason about.

2. **Why Favor Side-Effect-Free Functions?**

   - **Predictability**: Side-effect-free functions always produce the same output for the same input, regardless of external state.
   - **Parallelism**: Side-effect-free functions allow parallel execution without synchronization issues.
   - **Readability**: Code with minimal side effects is easier to understand and debug.

3. **Common Side Effects to Avoid**:

   - **Modifying State**: Functions that change the state of objects or variables.
   - **I/O Operations**: Functions that read from or write to files, databases, or the console.
   - **Printing**: Functions that print to the console.

4. **Examples of Side-Effect-Free Functions**:

   - map(): Transforms elements without modifying the original collection.
   - filter(): Selects elements based on a condition.
   - collect(): Aggregates elements into a new collection.
   - reduce(): Combines elements into a single result.

5. **Example Using Side-Effect-Free Functions**:

```
List<String> words = List.of("apple", "banana", "cherry");

// Side-effect-free: Transforming words to uppercase
List<String> uppercaseWords = words.stream()
    .map(String::toUpperCase)
    .collect(Collectors.toList());

System.out.println(uppercaseWords);
```

6. **Avoid Side Effects in Custom Functions**:

   - When writing custom functions for stream operations, ensure they don't modify external state.
   - If you need to perform side effects (e.g., logging), separate them from the main stream pipeline.

Remember that side-effect-free functions contribute to code reliability and maintainability. By adhering to this principle, you'll create more robust and predictable stream-based code!

○ **Returning Collections vs. Streams**

When designing APIs or writing methods that return data, you have the option to return either a collection (such as a List, Set, or Map) or a stream (from the java.util.stream.Stream API). Each approach has its advantages and use cases:

1. **Returning a Collection**:

   - **Advantages**:
     - **Mutability**: Collections allow modification of elements (e.g., adding or removing items) after retrieval.
     - **Immediate Materialization**: The entire collection is built up-front, providing a consistent snapshot of the data.
     - **Predictable Behavior**: Consumers can rely on the returned data not changing.
   - **Use Cases**:
     - When strong consistency requirements exist (e.g., producing a consistent snapshot of a moving target).
     - When the consumer needs to modify the data (e.g., add or remove elements).

2. **Returning a Stream**:

   - **Advantages**:
     - **Lazy Evaluation**: Streams are evaluated only when necessary (e.g., during iteration), which can improve performance.
     - **Parallelism**: Streams support parallel processing, distributing work across multiple threads.
     - **Functional Composition**: Streams allow chaining of operations (e.g., map, filter, reduce) in a declarative manner.
   - **Use Cases**:
     - When the consumer only needs to process the data (e.g., filtering, mapping, or aggregating).
     - When memory efficiency is critical (since streams don't materialize the entire collection).

Example Scenarios

1. **Returning a Collection**:

   - If your API provides a list of user profiles, and clients need to add or remove profiles, returning a List<User> is appropriate.
   - Similarly, when returning a set of configuration options, a Set<ConfigOption> allows modification.

2. **Returning a Stream**:

- If your API provides a large dataset (e.g., search results), returning a stream allows lazy evaluation and efficient processing.
- When dealing with infinite data sources (e.g., sensor readings), streams are suitable for handling data as it arrives.

Remember that the choice between collections and streams depends on the specific requirements of your use case. Consider factors such as mutability, consistency, and performance when deciding which type to return!

When using parallel streams in Java, it's essential to exercise caution and understand the implications. Parallel streams allow concurrent execution of operations, potentially improving performance on multi-core systems. However, there are considerations to keep in mind:

1. **Thread Safety**:

    - Parallel streams divide the data into chunks and process them concurrently using multiple threads.
    - Ensure that your data and operations are thread-safe. Avoid shared mutable state to prevent race conditions.

2. **Statelessness**:

    - Operations performed in parallel should be stateless (i.e., not rely on external state).
    - Avoid modifying external variables or objects within parallel stream operations.

3. **Overhead**:

    - Parallelism introduces overhead due to thread management, synchronization, and chunking.
    - For small datasets or lightweight operations, sequential streams may be more efficient.

4. **Ordering**:

    - Parallel streams do not guarantee the order of processing.
    - If order matters (e.g., when collecting results), consider using forEachOrdered() or other ordered operations.

5. **Load Balancing**:

    - The default parallelism level is based on the available processors (Runtime.getRuntime().availableProcessors()).
    - Adjust the parallelism level using parallelStream(n) if needed.

6. **Avoid Blocking Operations**:

    - Avoid blocking operations (e.g., I/O, waiting, or sleeping) within parallel streams.
    - Blocking one thread can impact the entire parallel execution.

Example of using parallel streams cautiously:

```
List<Integer> numbers = List.of(1, 2, 3, 4, 5, 6, 7, 8, 9, 10);

// Correct: Stateless operation (no external state)
int sum = numbers.parallelStream()
    .mapToInt(Integer::intValue)
    .sum();

// Incorrect: Modifying external state (avoid this)
List<Integer> result = new ArrayList<>();
numbers.parallelStream()
    .forEach(result::add); // Not thread-safe
```

```
System.out.println("Sum: " + sum);
```

In summary, parallel streams can significantly improve performance, but they require careful consideration. Use them judiciously, test thoroughly, and ensure thread safety for reliable results!

- **Exploring Techniques for Ensuring Validity of Method Input Parameters**

When writing robust and reliable Java code, validating method input parameters is crucial. Ensuring that the data passed to methods adheres to expected constraints helps prevent unexpected behavior, improves code quality, and enhances overall system reliability. In this article, we delve into various techniques for parameter validation in Java.

1. Traditional Null Checks

The most straightforward approach involves explicit null checks within the method body. For instance:

```java
public void myContractualMethod(String x, Set<String> y) {
    if (x == null || x.isEmpty()) {
        throw new IllegalArgumentException("x cannot be null or empty");
    }
    if (y == null) {
        throw new IllegalArgumentException("y cannot be null");
    }
    // Rest of the method logic
}
```

While effective, this approach can clutter the method implementation with boilerplate code, making it harder to focus on the core functionality.

2. Leveraging Google Guava Preconditions

Google Guava provides a concise way to validate parameters using its Preconditions class. By statically importing methods like checkNotNull and checkArgument, we can simplify our code:

```java
import com.google.common.base.Preconditions;

public void myContractualMethod(String x, Set<String> y) {
    Preconditions.checkNotNull(x);
    Preconditions.checkArgument(!x.isEmpty());
    Preconditions.checkNotNull(y);
    // Rest of the method logic
}
```

Guava's Preconditions library streamlines parameter validation and keeps the method body cleaner.

3. Custom Contract Classes

Create custom contract classes to encapsulate parameter validation logic. For example:

```java
package com.example;
```

```java
public class Contract {
    public static void isNotNull(Object obj) {
        if (obj == null) {
            throw new IllegalArgumentException("Illegal null");
        }
    }
}
```

Then use it in your method:

```java
public void myContractualMethod(String x, Set<String> y) {
    Contract.isNotNull(x);
    Contract.isNotNull(y);
    // Rest of the method logic
}
```

This approach promotes reusability and readability.

4. Parameter Annotations and Reflection

While Java annotations like JSR 303/Bean Validation Spec are primarily intended for annotating instance variables, we can creatively use them for method parameters. Although annotations won't directly enforce constraints, we can combine them with reflection to build a generic validator class that validates method parameters based on annotations.

Choose the technique that best suits your project's needs. Whether you opt for traditional null checks, leverage external libraries, or create custom contract classes, ensuring parameter validity is essential for writing robust and maintainable Java code. Remember that runtime exceptions (like IllegalArgumentExceptions) maintain encapsulation while providing clear feedback to developers.

Let's delve into practical approaches for enhancing code reliability and maintainability when it comes to validating method input parameters in Java. We'll explore techniques ranging from traditional null checks to modern annotations and design-by-contract frameworks.

1. Traditional Null Checks

The most straightforward approach involves explicit null checks within the method body. For instance:

```java
public void myContractualMethod(String x, Set<String> y) {
    if (x == null || x.isEmpty()) {
        throw new IllegalArgumentException("x cannot be null or empty");
    }
    if (y == null) {
        throw new IllegalArgumentException("y cannot be null");
    }
    // Rest of the method logic
}
```

While effective, this approach can clutter the method implementation with boilerplate code, making it harder to focus on the core functionality.

2. Leveraging Google Guava Preconditions

Google Guava provides a concise way to validate parameters using its Preconditions class. By statically importing methods like checkNotNull and checkArgument, we can simplify our code:

```
import com.google.common.base.Preconditions;

public void myContractualMethod(String x, Set<String> y) {
   Preconditions.checkNotNull(x);
   Preconditions.checkArgument(!x.isEmpty());
   Preconditions.checkNotNull(y);
   // Rest of the method logic
}
```

Guava's Preconditions library streamlines parameter validation and keeps the method body cleaner.

3. Custom Contract Classes

Create custom contract classes to encapsulate parameter validation logic. For example:

```
package com.example;

public class Contract {
   public static void isNotNull(Object obj) {
      if (obj == null) {
         throw new IllegalArgumentException("Illegal null");
      }
   }
}
```

Then use it in your method:

```
public void myContractualMethod(String x, Set<String> y) {
   Contract.isNotNull(x);
   Contract.isNotNull(y);
   // Rest of the method logic
}
```

This approach promotes reusability and readability.

4. Parameter Annotations and Reflection

While Java annotations like JSR 303/Bean Validation Spec are primarily intended for annotating instance variables, we can creatively use them for method parameters. Although annotations won't directly enforce constraints, we can combine them with reflection to build a generic validator class that validates method parameters based on annotations.

Choose the technique that best suits your project's needs. Whether you opt for traditional null checks, leverage external libraries, or create custom contract classes, ensuring parameter validity is essential for writing robust and maintainable Java code. Remember that runtime exceptions (like IllegalArgumentExceptions) maintain encapsulation while providing clear feedback to developers.

- **Creating Defensive Copies in Java: Best Practices and Examples**

What Is Defensive Copying?

Defensive copying is a programming practice where you create a **copy of an object** (usually a mutable one) to protect it from unintended modifications. Instead of directly exposing the original object, you provide a **safe, read-only copy** to other parts of your code.

Why Is It Important?

1. **Immutability and Consistency:**

   - By using defensive copies, you ensure that the state of an object remains **consistent** throughout its lifetime.
   - Immutable objects are inherently thread-safe and prevent unexpected changes.

2. **Avoiding Side Effects:**

   - When passing objects between methods or classes, defensive copies prevent **side effects**.
   - Without defensive copying, modifications made to shared objects can lead to unexpected behavior.

3. **API Design and Contracts:**

   - Defensive copying is crucial for designing robust APIs.
   - By returning defensive copies from methods, you define clear **contracts** about the mutability of objects.

4. **Security and Encapsulation:**

   - Sensitive data (e.g., passwords, private keys) should be defensively copied to prevent accidental exposure.
   - Encapsulation principles are reinforced by using defensive copies.

Examples:
- Suppose you have a Person class with a DateOfBirth field. To avoid exposing the original DateOfBirth object, return a defensive copy when accessing it.
- When dealing with collections (e.g., List, Map), create defensive copies to prevent external modifications.

Remember, defensive copying promotes **code correctness**, **maintainability**, and **reliable behavior**. It's a powerful tool in your Java programming toolbox!

Let's explore scenarios where defensive copies are essential and common use cases for creating them in Java:

Identifying Scenarios Requiring Defensive Copies:

1. **Mutable Fields in Immutable Objects:**

   - When designing an **immutable class**, ensure that any mutable fields (e.g., collections, arrays) are defensively copied.
   - Example: If your Person class has a List<String> representing phone numbers, return a defensive copy to prevent external modifications.

2. **Method Parameters and Return Values:**

   - When passing objects as method parameters or returning them from methods, consider defensive copying.
   - Avoid unintentional side effects caused by modifying shared objects.
   - Example: If a method accepts a Date object, create a defensive copy inside the method.

3. **Collections and Iterators:**

   - Collections (e.g., List, Set, Map) often need defensive copies.
   - When returning a collection from a method, return a copy to prevent modification.
   - Iterators should also work on a snapshot of the collection to avoid concurrent modification exceptions.

4. **Thread Safety and Concurrency:**

   - In multithreaded environments, defensive copying helps prevent race conditions.
   - Immutable objects are inherently thread-safe.
   - Example: When sharing data across threads, use defensive copies.

Common Use Cases for Creating Defensive Copies:

1. **String Manipulation:**

   - When working with strings, create defensive copies to avoid unintentional modifications.
   - Example: If you receive a String parameter, create a new String instance instead of modifying the original.

2. **Custom Value Objects:**

   - For custom value objects (e.g., Point, Color), use copy constructors or factory methods to create defensive copies.
   - Ensure that the original object remains unchanged.
   - Example: Implement a Point class with a copy constructor.

3. **Immutable Wrapper Classes:**

- Use wrapper classes (e.g., Integer, Double) for primitive types.
- These wrapper classes are immutable and provide defensive copies.
- Example: When passing an Integer parameter, it's already a defensive copy.

Remember, defensive copying promotes code reliability, prevents unintended side effects, and contributes to robust software design. Choose wisely based on your specific use case!

Let's dive into creating immutable objects in Java, including best practices and examples:

Designing Immutable Classes:

1. **Declare the Class as final:**

- To prevent subclassing and maintain immutability, declare your class as final.
- Child classes won't be able to modify the behavior of your immutable class.

2. **Private Data Members:**

- Declare all data members (fields) as private.
- This restricts direct access and modification from outside the class.

3. **Final Fields:**

- Mark data members as final.
- Once initialized, their values cannot change.

4. **Deep Copy in Constructors:**

- In the constructor, create a deep copy of any mutable objects passed as parameters.
- Ensure that the original object remains unaffected.

5. **No Setters:**

- Avoid providing setters for instance variables.
- Immutability means no changes after creation.

Example: Creating an Immutable Student Class

```java
import java.util.HashMap;
import java.util.Map;

final class Student {
    private final String name;
    private final int regNo;
    private final Map<String, String> metadata;
```

```java
    public Student(String name, int regNo, Map<String, String> metadata) {
        this.name = name;
        this.regNo = regNo;
        // Deep copy of metadata
        Map<String, String> tempMap = new HashMap<>();
        for (Map.Entry<String, String> entry : metadata.entrySet()) {
            tempMap.put(entry.getKey(), entry.getValue());
        }
        this.metadata = tempMap;
    }

    public String getName() {
        return name;
    }

    public int getRegNo() {
        return regNo;
    }

    public Map<String, String> getMetadata() {
        // Deep copy of metadata for safe access
        Map<String, String> tempMap = new HashMap<>();
        for (Map.Entry<String, String> entry : this.metadata.entrySet()) {
            tempMap.put(entry.getKey(), entry.getValue());
        }
        return tempMap;
    }
}

public class Main {
    public static void main(String[] args) {
        Map<String, String> map = new HashMap<>();
        map.put("1", "first");
        map.put("2", "second");

        Student s = new Student("ABC", 101, map);

        System.out.println(s.getName()); // ABC
        System.out.println(s.getRegNo()); // 101
        System.out.println(s.getMetadata()); // {1=first, 2=second}

        // Modifying the original map won't affect the student object
        map.put("3", "third");
        System.out.println(s.getMetadata()); // {1=first, 2=second}
    }
}
```

In this example, we've created an immutable Student class with deep copying of metadata.

Let's explore the concept of copy constructors in Java and how they help create defensive copies while ensuring the original object remains protected.

What Is a Copy Constructor?

A **copy constructor** is a special constructor within a class that allows you to create a new object by copying the state of an existing object. It provides a way to create a **deep copy** of an object, ensuring that any mutable fields are duplicated rather than shared.

Implementing Copy Constructors for Custom Classes:

1. **Constructor Signature:**

   - A copy constructor typically has the same parameter list as the regular constructor.
   - It takes an instance of the same class as its argument.

2. **Creating a New Object:**

   - Inside the copy constructor, create a new object with the same properties as the original.
   - If the original object contains references to other objects (e.g., collections, custom classes), make sure to create deep copies of those references.

3. **Immutable Fields:**

   - Immutable fields (declared as final) can be directly assigned in the copy constructor.
   - They don't need deep copying since their values cannot change.

4. **Deep Copy for Mutable Fields:**

   - For mutable fields, create new instances (copies) instead of sharing references.
   - This prevents unintended modifications to the original object.

Example: Copy Constructor for a Point Class

Suppose we have a simple Point class representing a 2D point:

```
class Point {
  private final double x;
  private final double y;

  public Point(double x, double y) {
    this.x = x;
    this.y = y;
  }

  // Copy constructor
  public Point(Point other) {
    this.x = other.x;
    this.y = other.y;
  }
}
```

```java
    public double getX() {
        return x;
    }

    public double getY() {
        return y;
    }
}

public class Main {
    public static void main(String[] args) {
        Point originalPoint = new Point(3.0, 4.0);

        // Create a copy using the copy constructor
        Point copiedPoint = new Point(originalPoint);

        System.out.println("Original Point: (" + originalPoint.getX() + ", " + originalPoint.getY() + ")");
        System.out.println("Copied Point: (" + copiedPoint.getX() + ", " + copiedPoint.getY() + ")");
    }
}
```

In this example, the Point class has a copy constructor that creates a new Point object with the same coordinates as the original. Any modifications to the copied point won't affect the original point.

Remember to apply copy constructors judiciously to ensure data integrity and protect your objects from unintended changes!

Let's explore examples of defensive copying in Java, covering both mutable objects and collections:

1. Creating a Defensive Copy of Mutable Objects

Suppose we have a Person class with a mutable field representing their address:

```java
class Person {
    private String name;
    private Address address;

    public Person(String name, Address address) {
        this.name = name;
        this.address = address;
    }

    // Create a defensive copy of the address
    public Address getAddress() {
        return new Address(address.getStreet(), address.getCity(), address.getZipCode());
    }
}

class Address {
    private String street;
```

```
    private String city;
    private String zipCode;

    public Address(String street, String city, String zipCode) {
        this.street = street;
        this.city = city;
        this.zipCode = zipCode;
    }

    // Getters for street, city, and zipCode
}
```

In the Person class, we create a defensive copy of the address when accessing it. This ensures that modifications to the returned address won't affect the original person object.

2. Demonstrating Defensive Copying with a Simple Point Class

```
class Point {
    private final double x;
    private final double y;

    public Point(double x, double y) {
        this.x = x;
        this.y = y;
    }

    // Copy constructor for defensive copying
    public Point(Point other) {
        this.x = other.x;
        this.y = other.y;
    }

    public double getX() {
        return x;
    }

    public double getY() {
        return y;
    }
}
```

The Point class has a copy constructor that allows us to create a new point by copying the coordinates from an existing point. This ensures that modifications to the copied point won't affect the original point.

3. Handling Collections Using Defensive Copies

When dealing with collections (e.g., List, Map), consider defensive copying:

- **List Example:**

```java
import java.util.ArrayList;
import java.util.Collections;
import java.util.List;

public class Main {
    public static void main(String[] args) {
        List<String> originalList = new ArrayList<>();
        originalList.add("Apple");
        originalList.add("Banana");

        // Create a defensive copy of the list
        List<String> copiedList = Collections.unmodifiableList(new ArrayList<>(originalList));

        // Modifications to the copied list won't affect the original list
        copiedList.add("Cherry"); // Throws UnsupportedOperationException
    }
}
```

- **Map Example:**

```java
import java.util.HashMap;
import java.util.Collections;
import java.util.Map;

public class Main {
    public static void main(String[] args) {
        Map<String, Integer> originalMap = new HashMap<>();
        originalMap.put("Alice", 30);
        originalMap.put("Bob", 25);

        // Create a defensive copy of the map
        Map<String, Integer> copiedMap = Collections.unmodifiableMap(new HashMap<>(originalMap));

        // Modifications to the copied map won't affect the original map
        copiedMap.put("Charlie", 28); // Throws UnsupportedOperationException
    }
}
```

Remember, defensive copying ensures data integrity, prevents unintended changes, and contributes to robust software design.

- **Best Practices for Designing Method Signatures**

When designing method signatures in Java, thoughtful consideration is crucial. Let's delve into the topics you've highlighted:

1. Choose Method Names Thoughtfully:

- **Standard Naming Conventions (Item 38):** Adhering to established naming conventions ensures consistency and readability. For instance, use camelCase for method names and follow the Java naming conventions.
- **Clarity and Consistency:** Prioritize names that convey the purpose of the method clearly. Avoid ambiguous or misleading names.
- **Java Library APIs:** Refer to existing Java library methods as examples. Learn from their naming patterns and apply similar principles to your own methods.

Remember, well-chosen method names enhance code readability and maintainability.

Let's explore the topic of avoiding excessive convenience methods in Java:

2. Avoid Excessive Convenience Methods:

- **Purposeful Methods:** Each method in your class should have a clear purpose. Avoid adding methods that merely duplicate existing functionality or provide minor variations.
- **Complication and Maintenance:** Too many convenience methods can clutter your class, making it harder to understand and maintain. It can also lead to confusion for users of your class.
- **Interface Design:** When designing interfaces, be mindful of the number of methods you expose. Aim for a manageable set of methods that cover essential functionality without overwhelming implementers.

Remember, striking the right balance between convenience and simplicity is crucial for creating robust and user-friendly APIs.

Here are some resources you can explore for in-depth information on designing method signatures in Java:

1. **InformIT: Design Method Signatures Carefully**

   - This resource provides practical insights and best practices for creating effective method signatures. You'll find tips on naming conventions, parameter lists, and more. Read it here.

2. **Bito: Java Method Signature Examples**

   - Bito.ai offers examples and explanations of various Java method signatures. Dive into real-world scenarios and learn how to design robust and meaningful methods. Explore it here.

3. **FavTutor: In-Depth Review of Method Signatures in Java**

   - FavTutor's article provides a comprehensive review of method signatures, covering essential concepts and common pitfalls. Enhance your understanding of this critical aspect of Java programming. Read it here.

Let's explore the topic of **keeping parameter lists concise** when designing method signatures in Java:

3. Keep Parameter Lists Concise:

- **Practical Maximum of Three Parameters:** Aim to limit the number of parameters in a method to a practical maximum of three. Beyond this, readability and maintainability suffer.
- **Challenges of Long Parameter Lists:**
  - **Memory Load:** Long parameter lists are harder to remember, especially when invoking methods across different parts of your codebase.
  - **Transposition Errors:** With many parameters, it's easier to accidentally swap their order, leading to subtle bugs.
- **Strategies for Managing Parameters:**
  - **Method Decomposition:** Consider breaking down complex methods into smaller, more focused ones. Each method should have a clear responsibility.
  - **Orthogonality:** Increase the orthogonality of your methods. In other words, ensure that each parameter serves a distinct purpose and doesn't overlap with others.

Remember, concise parameter lists contribute to code clarity and ease of use.

For further insights, refer to the resources mentioned earlier:

Here are some resources you can explore for in-depth information on designing method signatures in Java:

1. **InformIT: Design Method Signatures Carefully**

   - This resource provides practical insights and best practices for creating effective method signatures. You'll find tips on naming conventions, parameter lists, and more. Read it here.

2. **Bito: Java Method Signature Examples**

   - Bito.ai offers examples and explanations of various Java method signatures. Dive into real-world scenarios and learn how to design robust and meaningful methods. Explore it here.

3. **FavTutor: In-Depth Review of Method Signatures in Java**

   - FavTutor's article provides a comprehensive review of method signatures, covering essential concepts and common pitfalls. Enhance your understanding of this critical aspect of Java programming. Read it here.

Let's delve into the fascinating world of **method overloading** in Java.

Mastering Method Overloading in Java: Best Practices and Pitfalls

1. What Is Method Overloading?

Method overloading is a fundamental concept in Java that allows you to define **multiple methods with the same name** within a class. However, these methods must have **different parameter lists** (i.e., different types or different numbers of parameters). When you call an overloaded method, the appropriate version is chosen based on the method's signature at **compile time**.

2. Method Signature and Overloading Rules:

Understanding the rules of method overloading is crucial. Here are the key points:

- **Different Parameter Types:**

  - You can overload a method by varying the types of its parameters. For example:

    ```
    void print(int value) { /* ... */ }
    void print(double value) { /* ... */ }
    ```

- **Different Parameter Counts:**

  - Overloaded methods can have a different number of parameters. For instance:

    ```
    void greet(String name) { /* ... */ }
    void greet(String name, String title) { /* ... */ }
    ```

- **Combination of Both:**

  - You can combine different parameter types and counts:

    ```
    void process(int id) { /* ... */ }
    void process(String name, int age) { /* ... */ }
    ```

- **Maintaining Distinct Signatures:**

  - The key is to ensure that the method signatures remain distinct. The return type alone doesn't affect overloading.

3. Common Use Cases for Method Overloading:

Let's explore scenarios where method overloading shines:

- **Constructors with Different Parameter Sets:**

  - Constructors can be overloaded to create objects with varying initializations.
  - Example:

    ```
    public class Person {
        public Person(String name) { /* ... */ }
        public Person(String name, int age) { /* ... */ }
    }
    ```

- **Utility Methods with Varying Input Types:**

  - Overloading allows you to provide convenience methods for different data types.
  - Example:

    ```
    public class MathUtils {
        public static int add(int a, int b) { /* ... */ }
        public static double add(double a, double b) { /* ... */ }
    }
    ```

- **Convenience Methods for Handling Default Values:**

  - Overloaded methods can simplify parameter handling.
  - Example:

    ```
    public class StringUtils {
        public static String repeat(String str, int times) { /* ... */ }
        public static String repeat(String str) { /* ... */ } // Default times = 1
    }
    ```

4. Pitfalls and Considerations:

While method overloading is powerful, it comes with potential pitfalls:

- **Ambiguity:**

  - Be cautious when choosing parameter types to avoid ambiguity.
  - Compiler should be able to resolve the correct method unambiguously.

- **Static Type Resolution:**

  - Remember that method resolution happens at compile time based on static types.
  - Dynamic runtime types don't affect method selection.

- **"Use Overloading Judiciously":**

  - Follow Joshua Bloch's advice from "Effective Java."
  - Don't overload excessively; keep it clear and intuitive.

5. Best Practices:

Here are some best practices for effective method overloading:

- **Choose Parameter Types Carefully:**

    - Opt for meaningful parameter types to avoid confusion.
    - Clear method names enhance readability.

- **Consistent Behavior Across Overloaded Methods:**

    - Ensure that overloaded methods behave consistently.
    - Users should expect similar behavior regardless of the version they call.

- **Document the Purpose of Each Overloaded Method:**

    - Javadoc comments help users understand the differences.
    - Explain when to use each variant.

6. Real-World Examples:

Explore real-world scenarios where method overloading is indispensable:

- **Custom Data Structures:**

    - Implementing collections (e.g., ArrayList) with various constructors.
    - Providing flexibility to users.

- **User-Friendly APIs:**

    - Creating APIs with intuitive method names.
    - Enhancing developer experience.

Method overloading is a valuable tool, but like any tool, use it thoughtfully. By following best practices and understanding the rules, you'll wield method overloading effectively while maintaining code clarity and reliability.

Let's dive deeper into the rules and considerations for method overloading in Java.

Method Signature and Overloading Rules:

1. **Different Parameter Types:**

    - Method overloading allows you to define multiple methods with the same name but different parameter types.
    - For example:

    ```
    void print(int value) { /* ... */ }
    void print(double value) { /* ... */ }
    ```

- Here, we have two print methods—one accepting an int and the other a double.

2. **Different Parameter Counts:**

   - Overloaded methods can have a different number of parameters.
   - Example:

     ```
     void greet(String name) { /* ... */ }
     void greet(String name, String title) { /* ... */ }
     ```

   - In this case, the first method takes a single String argument, while the second method takes two String arguments.

3. **Combination of Both:**

   - You can combine different parameter types and counts:

     ```
     void process(int id) { /* ... */ }
     void process(String name, int age) { /* ... */ }
     ```

   - Here, we have two process methods—one with an int parameter and the other with a String and an int.

4. **Maintaining Distinct Signatures:**

   - The key to successful method overloading is ensuring that the method signatures remain distinct.
   - The return type alone doesn't affect overloading.
   - For example, the following is valid:

     ```
     int add(int a, int b) { /* ... */ }
     double add(double a, double b) { /* ... */ }
     ```

     Both methods have different parameter types (int vs. double), maintaining distinct signatures.

Importance of Clear Signatures:

- Clear and unambiguous method signatures are crucial:
  - The compiler must be able to resolve the correct method unambiguously.
  - Avoid situations where multiple overloaded methods could match the same arguments.

Remember, method overloading provides flexibility, but using it judiciously ensures code clarity and predictability.

Let's delve into the **common use cases for method overloading** in Java. Method overloading is a powerful technique that allows us to define multiple methods with the same name but different parameter lists. Here are some practical scenarios where method overloading proves beneficial:

1. **Constructors with Different Parameter Sets**:

   - When designing a class, you often need to create multiple constructors to initialize objects in various ways. Method overloading allows you to define constructors with different parameter lists. For example:

```java
public class Person {
    private String name;
    private int age;

    // Constructor with name and age
    public Person(String name, int age) {
        this.name = name;
        this.age = age;
    }

    // Constructor with only name (default age)
    public Person(String name) {
        this(name, 0); // Call the other constructor with default age
    }
}
```

   In this example, we have two constructors—one that takes both a name and an age, and another that only takes a name. The second constructor defaults the age to 0.

2. **Utility Methods with Varying Input Types**:

   - Suppose you're building a utility class that performs mathematical operations. Overloading allows you to handle different data types seamlessly. For instance:

```java
public class MathUtils {
    public static int add(int a, int b) {
        return a + b;
    }

    public static double add(double a, double b) {
        return a + b;
    }
}
```

   Here, we have overloaded the add method to work with both integers and doubles. Depending on the input types, the appropriate version of the method is invoked.

3. **Convenience Methods for Handling Default Values**:

   - Overloading can simplify method calls by providing default values for certain parameters. Consider a logging utility:

```java
public class Logger {
    public void log(String message) {
        // Log the message
```

```
            }

            public void log(String message, LogLevel level) {
                // Log the message with the specified level
            }

            public void log(String message, String category) {
                // Log the message with the given category
            }
        }
```

In this example, we've overloaded the log method to allow users to provide either a message, a message with a log level, or a message with a specific category.

Remember that method overloading enhances code readability and flexibility. It's a valuable tool in your Java programming toolbox!

Let's explore some **pitfalls and considerations** related to method overloading in Java, along with insights from Joshua Bloch's "Effective Java."

1. **Ambiguity When Choosing the Right Method**:

   - One of the challenges with method overloading is that it can lead to ambiguity. When multiple overloaded methods have similar parameter types, the compiler may struggle to determine which method to invoke. For example:

```
public class Calculator {
    public int add(int a, int b) {
        return a + b;
    }

    public double add(double a, double b) {
        return a + b;
    }
}
```

   In this scenario, if you call add(5, 5), the compiler won't know whether to use the int or double version. To avoid ambiguity, choose method names and parameter types carefully.

2. **Unexpected Behavior Due to Static Type Resolution**:

   - Method overloading is resolved at compile time (statically). The compiler determines which method to call based on the reference type, not the actual runtime type. Consider this example:

126

```java
public class Shape {
  public void draw() {
    System.out.println("Drawing a shape");
  }
}

public class Circle extends Shape {
  @Override
  public void draw() {
    System.out.println("Drawing a circle");
  }
}

public static void main(String[] args) {
  Shape shape = new Circle();
  shape.draw(); // Prints "Drawing a shape" (static type resolution)
}
```

Even though the actual object is a Circle, the method called is determined by the reference type (Shape). This can lead to unexpected behavior if you're not aware of the static resolution.

3. **The "Use Overloading Judiciously" Principle**:

   - Joshua Bloch emphasizes that method overloading should be used judiciously. Overloading can make code more complex and harder to understand. It's essential to strike a balance between flexibility and readability.
   - Consider the context, readability, and maintainability of your code. Avoid excessive overloading, especially when it leads to confusion.

In summary, method overloading is a powerful tool, but it requires thoughtful design. Be mindful of potential pitfalls, understand static type resolution, and follow best practices to create clean and maintainable code.

Let's explore some **best practices for using method overloading effectively** in Java:

1. **Choose Parameter Types Carefully to Avoid Ambiguity**:

   - When overloading methods, ensure that the parameter types are distinct enough to avoid confusion. If multiple overloaded methods have similar parameter lists, it can lead to ambiguity during method resolution.

   - For example, consider the following scenario:

```java
public class Calculator {
   public int add(int a, int b) {
      return a + b;
   }

   public double add(double a, double b) {
      return a + b;
   }
}
```

Here, calling add(5, 5) would be ambiguous because both int and double versions match. Be mindful of such cases and choose meaningful parameter types.

2. **Ensure Consistent Behavior Across Overloaded Methods**:

   • Overloaded methods should exhibit consistent behavior. Users expect similar functionality when invoking methods with the same name.
   • For instance, if you have an overloaded print method, ensure that regardless of the data type or parameters, the purpose (printing) remains consistent.

3. **Document the Purpose of Each Overloaded Method**:

   • Clear documentation is essential. Describe the purpose of each overloaded method, including the differences in parameter lists.
   • Javadoc comments or inline explanations help other developers understand the intent behind each method.

Remember that method overloading is a powerful tool, but it requires thoughtful design. By following these best practices, you can create clean, maintainable code that benefits from the flexibility of method overloading.

For further insights and detailed examples, I recommend referring to Joshua Bloch's book "Effective Java" (Item 41: "Use overloading judiciously").

- **Using Varargs Effectively: Best Practices and Considerations**

  What Are Varargs?

- **Varargs** (short for "variable-length argument lists") is a feature in Java that allows methods to accept an **arbitrary number of arguments** of the same type.
- It simplifies the process of passing multiple values to a method without explicitly specifying an array.
- Varargs are denoted by an ellipsis (...) after the parameter type in the method signature.

How Varargs Work:

1. **Declaration**:

   - To declare a method with varargs, use the following syntax:

   ```
   returnType methodName(type... parameterName) {
       // Method implementation
   }
   ```

2. **Usage**:

   - When calling a varargs method, you can provide any number of arguments (including zero) of the specified type.
   - The arguments are automatically packed into an array within the method.

3. **Example**:

   ```
   public class Calculator {
       public static int sum(int... numbers) {
           int total = 0;
           for (int num : numbers) {
               total += num;
           }
           return total;
       }

       public static void main(String[] args) {
           int result1 = sum(1, 2, 3); // Calls sum with an array {1, 2, 3}
           int result2 = sum(10, 20);  // Calls sum with an array {10, 20}
           int result3 = sum();        // Calls sum with an empty array
           System.out.println("Result: " + result1 + ", " + result2 + ", " + result3);
       }
   }
   ```

   In this example, the sum method accepts any number of int arguments and calculates their sum.

Benefits of Varargs:

- **Flexibility**: Varargs allow you to create methods that handle varying input sizes without explicitly defining an array.
- **Conciseness**: You can call varargs methods with a cleaner syntax, avoiding the need to create and pass arrays explicitly.

Remember to use varargs judiciously—consider readability, maintainability, and the purpose of your method. Varargs are a powerful tool when used appropriately!

Let's delve into the practical scenarios where **varargs** (short for "variable arguments") in Java come in handy. Varargs allow a method to accept an **indeterminate number of arguments**. Before varargs, we often used overloaded methods or arrays as method parameters, but varargs provide a more elegant solution.

When to Use Varargs: Practical Scenarios

1. **String.format**:

   - One of the most common use cases for varargs is in the String.format method. This method allows you to create formatted strings by replacing placeholders with actual values.
   - The format string can accept any number of parameters, so varargs simplify passing multiple arguments to format strings. For example:

     String formattedString1 = String.format("This is an integer: %d", myInt);
     String formattedString2 = String.format("This is an integer: %d and a string: %s", myInt, myString);

2. **Other Core APIs**:

   - Beyond String.format, varargs are useful in other core APIs as well.
   - **Reflection**: When invoking methods using reflection, varargs allow you to pass an arbitrary number of arguments to the method being invoked.
   - **Message Formatting**: In scenarios where you need to construct messages dynamically (e.g., logging or internationalization), varargs simplify handling different message components.
   - **printf-Style Methods**: Methods that follow the printf pattern (such as System.out.printf) benefit from varargs. These methods allow you to format and print messages with placeholders and corresponding values.

Rules for Using Varargs:

1. There can be **only one** variable argument (varargs) in a method.
2. The varargs parameter **must be the last argument** in the method signature.
3. Be aware of **heap pollution**, which can occur when using varargs.

Remember, varargs provide flexibility and convenience, allowing you to handle an **unknown number of arguments** effectively. So embrace them when dealing with dynamic scenarios!

Here are some best practices for using **varargs** in Java:

1. **Clear Documentation**:

   - When designing methods that accept varargs, provide clear and concise documentation. Explain how the method handles the variable number of arguments and any specific rules or constraints.
   - Users of your method will appreciate well-documented behavior, especially when dealing with varargs.

2. **Avoid Excessive Reliance on Varargs**:

   - While varargs are powerful, don't overuse them. Relying too heavily on varargs can lead to less readable code.
   - Consider whether an overloaded method or a different approach might improve code clarity. Sometimes explicit parameter lists are more intuitive than varargs.

3. **Understand Limitations and Behavior**:

   - Be aware of the rules for using varargs:
     - There can be **only one** variable argument (varargs) in a method.
     - The varargs parameter **must be the last argument** in the method signature.
   - Understand how varargs behave when passed an empty array or null values.
   - Be cautious of **heap pollution**, which can occur due to unchecked type safety when using varargs.

Remember, varargs provide flexibility, but like any tool, they should be used judiciously.

Here are some guidelines for API designers when it comes to using **varargs**:

1. **Use Varargs Sparingly**:

   - Only employ varargs when their benefit is truly compelling. Consider whether the flexibility they provide outweighs any potential downsides.
   - Overusing varargs can lead to code that is harder to read and maintain.

2. **Trade-offs Between Flexibility and Readability**:

   - Varargs offer flexibility by allowing an arbitrary number of arguments, but this can come at the cost of readability.
   - Weigh the trade-offs carefully. Sometimes explicit parameter lists or other design choices may be more intuitive and maintainable.

Remember, thoughtful API design contributes to better software development practices. Choose wisely!

• Best Practices: Returning Empty Collections or Arrays Instead of Null

Let's dive into the introduction for your post on returning empty collections or arrays instead of nulls in Java.

Introduction: The Null Dilemma in Java APIs

When designing APIs that involve collections or arrays, developers often face a common challenge: **how to handle method return values when no data is available**. The traditional approach has been to return null in such cases. However, this practice can lead to several issues:

1. **NullPointerExceptions (NPEs)**:

    • When client code receives a null result and attempts to access elements within it, an NPE may occur. These runtime exceptions can be hard to debug and cause unexpected program failures.

2. **Readability and Defensive Coding**:

    • Code that deals with null checks becomes cluttered and less readable. Developers must add conditional checks to handle null cases, which can obscure the main logic.
    • Defensive coding practices often involve explicit null checks, leading to boilerplate code.

3. **Inconsistent Behavior**:

    • Different methods returning null or empty values can confuse developers. Inconsistent behavior across APIs makes it challenging to predict how a method will behave.

To address these issues, we advocate for a better approach: **returning empty collections or arrays instead of null**. By doing so, we ensure meaningful and consistent behavior, simplify client code, and promote cleaner APIs. In the upcoming sections, we'll explore why this practice is beneficial and how to implement it effectively.

Let's delve into the drawbacks of returning null from methods and why it's beneficial to avoid this practice:

1. **Risk of NullPointerExceptions (NPEs)**:

    • When a method returns null, client code that relies on the result is at risk of encountering NPEs.
    • An NPE occurs when an attempt is made to access a method or field on a null reference. These exceptions can crash the program or lead to unexpected behavior.
    • By returning empty collections or arrays instead of null, we eliminate this risk. Clients can safely iterate over empty structures without fear of NPEs.

2. Reduced Code Readability:

- Code that deals with null checks becomes less readable. Developers must add conditional statements to handle null cases.
- For example, consider the following snippet:

```
List<String> getNames() {
    // If no names are available, return null
    // Otherwise, return a list of names
}
// Client code:
List<String> names = getNames();
if (names != null) {
    // Process the list of names
}
```

- The null check adds noise to the code and distracts from the main logic.

3. Potential Confusion for Developers:

- Inconsistent behavior across APIs can confuse developers. Some methods return null, while others return empty collections or arrays.
- By adopting a consistent approach (preferably returning empties), we make our APIs more predictable and easier to use.

In summary, avoiding nulls in favor of empty structures leads to cleaner, safer code. Let's explore how to implement this best practice effectively!

Let's explore the benefits of returning empty collections or arrays instead of null in Java:

1. Avoiding NullPointerExceptions (NPEs):

- When a method returns an empty collection or array (e.g., an empty list, set, or array), it ensures that the result is always valid.
- Clients can safely iterate over empty structures without encountering NPEs. No more worrying about null references causing unexpected crashes!

2. Simplified Client Code:

- Returning empties simplifies client code. Developers no longer need to clutter their logic with null checks.
- Compare the following:

```
// Using null:
List<String> names = getNames();
if (names != null) {
    // Process the list of names
}

// Using an empty list:
List<String> names = getNames();
// No null check needed; proceed directly with processing
```

- The second approach is cleaner and easier to read.

3. **Consistent Behavior**:

    - By consistently returning empty collections or arrays, we establish predictable behavior across APIs.
    - Whether data exists or not, clients know they'll receive a valid structure. This consistency fosters better code maintenance and understanding.

In summary, embracing the practice of returning empties leads to safer, more readable code.

Let's explore some implementation techniques for returning empty collections or arrays in Java:

1. **Using Collections.emptyList()**:

    - The Collections class provides utility methods for creating empty collections.
    - To return an empty list, use Collections.emptyList():

    ```
    import java.util.Collections;
    import java.util.List;

    public class MyService {
       public List<String> getEmptyList() {
          return Collections.emptyList();
       }
    }
    ```

2. **Using Collections.emptySet()**:

    - Similarly, for empty sets, use Collections.emptySet():

    ```
    import java.util.Collections;
    import java.util.Set;

    public class MyService {
       public Set<Integer> getEmptySet() {
          return Collections.emptySet();
       }
    }
    ```

3. **Using Collections.emptyMap()**:

    - For empty maps, use Collections.emptyMap():

    ```
    import java.util.Collections;
    import java.util.Map;

    public class MyService {
       public Map<String, Integer> getEmptyMap() {
          return Collections.emptyMap();
       }
    }
    ```

4. **Creating an Empty Array Directly**:

- To return an empty array, simply create one directly:

```
public class MyService {
  public int[] getEmptyIntArray() {
    return new int[0];
  }
}
```

Remember, these techniques ensure that your methods consistently return valid, empty structures, promoting cleaner code and reducing the risk of NPEs.

Let's delve into some **performance considerations** in Java. Optimizing memory usage and performance is crucial for efficient software. Here are some relevant points:

1. **Collections.emptyList()**:

- When you need an empty list, consider using Collections.emptyList().
- It returns an **immutable** (read-only) list instance that is shared across all invocations.
- Benefits:
  - **Reduced memory overhead**: Since it's a singleton instance, no additional memory is allocated for empty lists.
  - **Avoids unnecessary object creation**: Creating a new empty list each time can be wasteful.
- Example:

```
List<String> emptyList = Collections.emptyList();
```

2. **Stack-Based Allocation for Empty Collections or Arrays**:

- Some JVMs optimize memory allocation for empty collections or arrays.
- Instead of heap allocation, they allocate these objects on the stack.
- Benefits:
  - **Faster allocation and deallocation**: Stack-based allocation is more efficient.
  - **Less pressure on garbage collection**: Stack-allocated objects don't contribute to heap memory.
- Note: This behavior may vary across JVM implementations.
- Example (hypothetical):

```
// Stack-allocated empty array
int[] emptyArray = new int[0];
```

Remember that these optimizations are subtle but can significantly impact performance, especially in resource-intensive applications.

When designing APIs, encouraging the use of empty collections or arrays can lead to more efficient and cleaner code. Here are some guidelines for API designers:

1. **Avoid Weakly Typed Collections**:

   - Instead of using generic collections like ArrayList or List<T>, prefer strongly typed collections.
   - Weakly typed collections can lead to runtime errors due to type mismatches.
   - Example:

     ```
     // Weakly typed (avoid)
     ArrayList myList = new ArrayList();
     myList.add("Hello");
     String value = (String) myList.get(0); // Requires casting

     // Strongly typed (prefer)
     List<String> myTypedList = new ArrayList<>();
     myTypedList.add("Hello");
     String typedValue = myTypedList.get(0); // No casting needed
     ```

2. **Prefer IEnumerable<T> or Custom Types**:

```
// Prefer using interfaces like List<T> or Set<T> (in Java) or custom types implementing Map<K, V> or Collection<E>.
// These interfaces provide better type safety and allow for more expressive code.

import java.util.List;
import java.util.ArrayList;
import java.util.Collection;

public class MyCustomCollection<T> implements Collection<T> {
    // Implement required methods for the Collection interface
    // (e.g., add, remove, contains, size, etc.).

    public static void main(String[] args) {
        // Example usage:
        List<String> myStrings = new ArrayList<>();
        myStrings.add("A");
        myStrings.add("B");
        myStrings.add("C");

        // Custom collection usage:
        MyCustomCollection<Integer> myCustomCollection = new MyCustomCollection<>();
        myCustomCollection.add(42);
        myCustomCollection.add(99);
        // ...

        // You can now use myStrings and myCustomCollection in your code.
    }
}
```

By adhering to these guidelines, API designers can create more robust and maintainable APIs that enhance developer productivity and reduce potential bugs.

Certainly! Let's dive into the **Introduction to Optional** in Java:

1. **Purpose of `Optional`**:

   - The `Optional` class was introduced in Java 8 to address the issue of dealing with **nullable** values.
   - It provides a **type-safe** alternative to using `null` references.
   - The goal is to make code more **readable**, **expressive**, and **safe** by explicitly handling the absence of a value.

2. **Why Avoid `null`?**:

   - `null` is a common source of **NullPointerExceptions** (NPEs) in Java programs.
   - It lacks type information, making it error-prone and hard to reason about.
   - `Optional` encourages developers to be more deliberate about handling absent values.

3. **Key Features of `Optional`**:

   - Represents an **optional** value that can be either present or absent.
   - Forces explicit handling of absence using methods like `orElse()`, `orElseGet()`, and `ifPresent()`.
   - Encourages better design by making nullability explicit in method signatures.

4. **Creating an `Optional`**:

   - Use `Optional.of(value)` to create an `Optional` with a non-null value.
   - Use `Optional.ofNullable(value)` to create an `Optional` from a nullable value (handles `null` gracefully).
   - Example:

   ```
   Optional<String> maybeName =
   Optional.ofNullable(getNameFromDatabase());
   ```

5. **Common Use Cases**:

   - **Method Return Types**: Use `Optional` as a return type for methods that may not always produce a result.
   - **Stream Processing**: `Optional` integrates well with Java streams for handling optional elements.
   - **Avoiding `null` Checks**: Replace cumbersome `if (value != null)` checks with `ifPresent()`.

6. **When Not to Use `Optional`**:

   - Avoid returning `Optional` for simple getters in POJOs (Plain Old Java Objects).
   - Use `Optional` judiciously; not every method needs to return an `Optional`.

- ## Mastering Optional Return Types: Best Practices and Pitfalls

Let's delve into scenarios where returning an Optional is appropriate and how to use it effectively:

1. **Database Lookups**:

   - When querying a database or external service, the result may not always exist.
   - Instead of returning null, use Optional to indicate the absence of a value.
   - Example:

   ```
   public Optional<User> findUserByName(String username) {
       // Query database and return an Optional<User>
       // If user not found, return Optional.empty()
   }
   ```

2. **Utility Methods**:

   - Utility methods often deal with optional values.
   - For instance, a utility method that parses an integer from a string:

   ```
   public Optional<Integer> parseInteger(String input) {
       try {
           int value = Integer.parseInt(input);
           return Optional.of(value);
       } catch (NumberFormatException e) {
           return Optional.empty();
       }
   }
   ```

3. **Static Factory Methods**:

   - Static factory methods can return Optional instances.
   - For example, a method that reads a configuration property:

   ```
   public static Optional<String> readConfigProperty(String key) {
       // Read property value; return Optional.of(value) or Optional.empty()
   }
   ```

4. **Avoiding Null Checks**:

   - Returning Optional encourages developers to handle absence explicitly.
   - It eliminates the need for cumbersome if (result != null) checks.
   - Developers can use methods like orElse(), orElseGet(), or ifPresent().

Remember, using Optional judiciously improves code clarity and helps prevent null-related bugs. Choose it wisely based on the specific context of your application!

1. **Creating Optional Instances**:

   - Use Optional.ofNullable(value) to create an Optional from a nullable value.
   - Example:

     ```
     String nullableValue = ...; // Some nullable value
     Optional<String> optionalValue = Optional.ofNullable(nullableValue);
     ```

2. **Avoid Returning Optional for Simple Getters**:

   - While Optional is useful for methods that may not always produce a result, avoid using it for simple getters.
   - For instance, don't return an Optional<String> for a getName() method in a POJO (Plain Old Java Object).
   - Instead, return the actual value or null directly.

3. **Serialization Challenges**:

   - When serializing objects containing Optional fields (e.g., to JSON), consider the following:
     - Some serialization libraries handle Optional automatically (e.g., Jackson).
     - Others may require custom serializers or handling.
     - Be aware of how Optional fields affect the resulting JSON structure.

4. **JSON Serialization Implications**:

   - If an Optional field is empty (Optional.empty()), some libraries may omit it during serialization.
   - If you want to include the field even when empty, handle it explicitly.
   - Example (using Jackson):

     ```
     @JsonInclude(JsonInclude.Include.ALWAYS)
     private Optional<String> myField = Optional.empty();
     ```

Remember that using Optional thoughtfully improves code readability and helps prevent null-related issues. Choose it wisely based on your specific use cases!

Let's explore some common pitfalls and anti-patterns related to using Optional in Java. Avoiding these will lead to cleaner and more maintainable code:

Common Pitfalls and Anti-Patterns with Optional in Java

1. **Overusing Optional**:

   - **Issue**: Not every method needs to return an Optional.
   - **Why It's a Pitfall**:

- Overusing Optional can make the code verbose and less readable.
- It may lead to unnecessary complexity, especially for simple scenarios.
- **Guidelines**:
  - Use Optional judiciously. Consider whether returning an Optional truly adds value.
  - For methods that always produce a result, prefer returning the actual value or null.

2. **Nesting Optional<Optional<T>>**:

- **Issue**: Nesting Optional within another Optional.
- **Why It's a Pitfall**:
  - It introduces unnecessary complexity and confusion.
  - Handling nested optionals requires additional unwrapping steps.
- **Guidelines**:
  - Avoid nesting Optional. If a method already returns an Optional, don't wrap its result in another Optional.
  - Flatten nested optionals using methods like flatMap().

3. **Balancing Readability and Null Safety**:

- **Issue**: Choosing between null safety and code readability.
- **Why It's a Pitfall**:
  - Prioritizing null safety can lead to overly verbose code.
  - Prioritizing readability may overlook null-related issues.
- **Guidelines**:
  - Aim for a balance:
    - Use Optional where it enhances readability and expresses intent.
    - Be cautious not to sacrifice readability for the sake of null safety.
  - Consider using orElse() or orElseGet() for concise fallback values.

Remember that Optional is a powerful tool, but like any tool, it should be used thoughtfully. Strive for clarity, simplicity, and maintainability in your code!

Handling Optional in Practice

The Optional class, introduced in Java 8, provides a powerful solution for dealing with potentially absent values. It helps us avoid the dreaded NullPointerExceptions and simplifies null-checking logic. In this article, we'll explore various techniques for working with Optional.

1. Overview

The primary purpose of the Optional class is to represent optional values instead of using null references. Here are some key points to consider:

- **Why Use Optional?** It encourages a type-level approach to handling optional values, making our code safer and cleaner.
- **Creating Optional Objects:**
  - To create an empty Optional, use the empty() static method:

    ```
    Optional<String> empty = Optional.empty();
    assertFalse(empty.isPresent());
    ```

  - To create an Optional with a non-null value, use Optional.of():

    ```
    String name = "baeldung";
    Optional<String> opt = Optional.of(name);
    assertTrue(opt.isPresent());
    ```

  - If you expect null values, use Optional.ofNullable():

    ```
    String nullableName = null;
    Optional<String> nullableOpt = Optional.ofNullable(nullableName);
    assertFalse(nullableOpt.isPresent());
    ```

- **Checking Value Presence:**
  - Use isPresent() to check if a value exists:

    ```
    Optional<String> baeldungOpt = Optional.of("Baeldung");
    assertTrue(baeldungOpt.isPresent());
    ```

    ```
    Optional<String> nullOpt = Optional.ofNullable(null);
    assertFalse(nullOpt.isPresent());
    ```

2. Common Methods

Let's explore some common methods for working with Optional:

a. orElse() vs. orElseGet()

- orElse() returns the wrapped value if present, or a default value if absent:

  ```
  String result = baeldungOpt.orElse("Default Value");
  ```

- orElseGet() accepts a Supplier to provide the default value lazily:

  ```
  String result = baeldungOpt.orElseGet(() -> expensiveComputation());
  ```

b. Filtering Streams of Optionals

- When working with streams of Optional values, use filter():

  ```
  List<Optional<String>> optionalList = // ...
  ```

  ```
  List<String> nonEmptyValues = optionalList.stream()
  ```

```
.filter(Optional::isPresent)
.map(Optional::get)
.collect(Collectors.toList());
```

c. Combining Optionals Elegantly

- Use flatMap() to combine multiple Optional values:

```
Optional<String> firstName = // ...
Optional<String> lastName = // ...

Optional<String> fullName = firstName.flatMap(fn ->
    lastName.map(ln -> fn + " " + ln)
);
```

By mastering the usage of Optional, we can write safer and more expressive code. Remember to choose Optional over explicit null checks whenever possible.

- ## Writing Effective Doc Comments for Java APIs

Understanding Doc Comments in Java

In the world of Java programming, **doc comments** play a crucial role in creating well-documented and maintainable APIs. These special comments provide essential information about classes, methods, fields, and other program elements. Let's dive into the details:

Purpose of Doc Comments

1. **Documentation for Developers:**

   - Doc comments serve as a form of documentation for developers who use your code. They explain how to use classes, methods, and other API elements effectively.
   - By reading doc comments, developers gain insights into the purpose, behavior, and usage of each element.

2. **API Usability:**

   - Well-written doc comments enhance the usability of your APIs. When others (or even your future self) interact with your code, clear documentation makes it easier to understand and utilize the available functionality.
   - APIs without proper documentation can be confusing and error-prone.

Difference from Regular Comments

- **Regular Comments:**

  - Regular comments (those starting with // or enclosed within /* ... */) are meant for human readers but are ignored by the compiler.
  - They provide context, explanations, or reminders within the code.
  - Example:

    ```
    // Calculate the total price
    double totalPrice = calculatePrice(quantity, unitPrice);
    ```

- **Doc Comments (Javadoc):**

  - Doc comments are specifically formatted comments recognized by the Javadoc tool.
  - They begin with /** and end with */.
  - Javadoc extracts information from these comments to generate API documentation.
  - Example:

    ```
    /**
     * Calculates the total price based on the given quantity and unit price.
     *
     * @param quantity   The quantity of items.
    ```

```
     * @param unitPrice  The price per unit.
     * @return The total price.
     */
    public double calculatePrice(int quantity, double unitPrice) {
        // Implementation details...
    }
```

Significance of Doc Comments

1. **Automated Documentation:**

   - Javadoc processes doc comments and generates HTML documentation files. These files include class overviews, method details, parameter descriptions, return values, and exceptions.
   - Developers can access this documentation directly or through tools like IDEs.

2. **Self-Explanatory APIs:**

   - Well-crafted doc comments make APIs self-explanatory. Users can understand how to call methods, what parameters to provide, and what to expect in return.
   - For example, when exploring a library, you'll appreciate clear doc comments that guide you through the available methods.

3. **Contract Clarity:**

   - Doc comments define the contract between the API provider (you) and the API consumer (other developers).
   - They specify method behavior, expected inputs, and possible exceptions.
   - When developers adhere to this contract, their code integrates seamlessly with your API.

In summary, writing comprehensive and accurate doc comments is essential for creating robust, user-friendly APIs. Take the time to document your code—it pays off in the long run!

Javadoc Utility: Unleashing the Power of Documentation

In the vast landscape of Java development, the **Javadoc utility** stands as a beacon for creating comprehensive and well-structured documentation. Let's explore what Javadoc is, how it works, and why it's an indispensable tool in the Java community.

What Is Javadoc?

- **Definition:** Javadoc is a tool bundled with the Java Development Kit (JDK) that automatically generates API documentation from specially formatted comments within your source code.
- **Purpose:** Its primary purpose is to create clear, informative, and consistent documentation for your classes, methods, fields, and other program elements.
- **Format:** Javadoc comments begin with /** and end with */. They reside directly above the code element they describe.

How Does Javadoc Work?

1. **Comment Extraction:**

   - Javadoc scans your source files, seeking out these special comments.
   - It extracts relevant information such as method descriptions, parameter details, return values, and exceptions.

2. **HTML Documentation Generation:**

   - Once collected, Javadoc processes this information and generates HTML files.
   - These files form the API documentation, complete with hyperlinks, cross-references, and organized sections.

3. **Standard Tags:**

   - Javadoc recognizes standard tags (prefixed with @) within comments.
   - Common tags include:
     - @param: Describes method parameters.
     - @return: Explains the return value.
     - @throws or @exception: Documents exceptions thrown by the method.

4. **Inheritance and Overriding:**

   - Javadoc also considers inheritance and method overriding.
   - If a subclass overrides a method, its Javadoc inherits from the superclass, but it can be further refined.

Why Is Javadoc Widely Used?

1. **API Clarity:**

   - Javadoc ensures that API users (including other developers) understand how to interact with your code.
   - It provides a clear contract, specifying method behavior and expectations.

2. **Integrated with IDEs:**

   - Most Integrated Development Environments (IDEs) support Javadoc.
   - Developers can hover over method names or use shortcuts to view Javadoc directly within their code editor.

3. **Standardization:**

   - Javadoc enforces a consistent format for documentation.
   - This consistency benefits both developers and consumers of your APIs.

4. **Automatic Updates:**

   - When you modify your code, regenerate the Javadoc, and the documentation stays up-to-date.
   - No manual effort required!

In the Java ecosystem, Javadoc isn't just a tool; it's a bridge connecting developers, libraries, and frameworks. By embracing Javadoc, you contribute to a culture of clarity, collaboration, and excellence. So, next time you write a method, remember to add those enlightening comments—your fellow developers will thank you!

Doc Comment Conventions in Java

When it comes to writing **doc comments** in Java, following conventions ensures that your documentation is consistent, informative, and useful for both developers and users of your APIs. Let's explore these conventions and provide examples of well-structured doc comments.

1. Preceding Every Exported Element

- **Rule:** Precede every exported class, interface, constructor, method, and field declaration with a doc comment.
- **Why?** This practice ensures that all significant elements are documented, making it easier for others to understand their purpose and usage.

Example (Method):

```
/**
 * Calculates the total price based on the given quantity and unit price.
 *
 * @param quantity   The quantity of items.
 * @param unitPrice  The price per unit.
 * @return The total price.
 * @throws IllegalArgumentException if quantity or unitPrice is negative.
 */
public double calculatePrice(int quantity, double unitPrice) {
    // Implementation details...
}
```

2. Enumerating @param Tags

- **Rule:** Enumerate all method parameters using @param tags within the doc comment.
- **Why?** Explicitly documenting each parameter helps users understand their purpose and expected values.

Example (Method with Parameters):

```
/**
 * Retrieves the user's profile based on the provided user ID.
 *
 * @param userId The unique identifier for the user.
 * @return The user's profile information.
 * @throws UserNotFoundException if the user with the given ID does not exist.
 */
public UserProfile getUserProfile(String userId) {
    // Implementation details... }
```

3. Documenting Preconditions, Postconditions, and Exceptions

- **Rule:** Use @throws tags to document exceptions that a method may throw.
- **Why?** Describing exceptions helps users handle potential errors gracefully.

Example (Method with Preconditions and Exceptions):

```
/**
 * Withdraws the specified amount from the user's account.
 *
 * @param accountId The account ID.
 * @param amount    The amount to withdraw (must be positive).
 * @throws InsufficientFundsException if the account balance is insufficient.
 * @throws IllegalArgumentException if the amount is non-positive.
 */
public void withdrawAmount(String accountId, double amount) {
    // Implementation details...
}
```

4. Using HTML Metacharacters and Tags

- **Rule:** Use HTML metacharacters (such as <code>, <em>, <ul>, etc.) for formatting within doc comments.
- **Why?** Proper formatting enhances readability and comprehension.

Example (Class with Description and List):

```
/**
 * Represents an online shopping cart.
 * <p>
 * This class provides methods for adding items, calculating the total price,
 * and checking out.
 * </p>
 * <p>
 * Example usage:
 * <ul>
 *   <li>Create a cart: {@code ShoppingCart cart = new ShoppingCart();}</li>
 *   <li>Add items: {@code cart.addItem(item1); cart.addItem(item2);}</li>
 *   <li>Calculate total: {@code double totalPrice = cart.calculateTotal();}</li>
 * </ul>
 * </p>
 */
public class ShoppingCart {
    // Implementation details...
}
```

Remember, well-structured doc comments serve as a bridge between your code and its users. By adhering to these conventions, you contribute to a more transparent and developer-friendly ecosystem.

Best Practices for Writing Effective Doc Comments in Java

When documenting your Java code, **doc comments** play a crucial role in conveying essential information to other developers and users of your APIs. Let's explore some best practices for creating clear and informative doc comments:

1. Focus on the Contract

- **Contract-Oriented Approach:**
  - When writing doc comments, focus on the contract between the method (or class) and its client.
  - Describe what the method does, its purpose, and its expected behavior.
  - Avoid diving into implementation details or low-level specifics.

Example (Method Contract):

```java
/**
 * Calculates the total price based on the given quantity and unit price.
 *
 * @param quantity   The quantity of items.
 * @param unitPrice  The price per unit.
 * @return The total price.
 * @throws IllegalArgumentException if quantity or unitPrice is negative.
 */
public double calculatePrice(int quantity, double unitPrice) {
    // Implementation details...
}
```

2. Descriptive Noun Phrases

- **Use Descriptive Nouns:**
  - For @param and @return tags, use descriptive noun phrases.
  - Clearly state what each parameter represents and what the method returns.

Example (Descriptive Noun Phrases):

```java
/**
 * Retrieves the user's profile based on the provided user ID.
 *
 * @param userId The unique identifier for the user.
 * @return The user's profile information.
 * @throws UserNotFoundException if the user with the given ID does not exist.
 */
public UserProfile getUserProfile(String userId) {
    // Implementation details...
}
```

3. Exception Conditions

- **Document Exception Conditions:**
    - Use @throws tags to specify exceptions that a method may throw.
    - Clearly state the conditions under which these exceptions occur.

Example (Exception Conditions):

```
/**
 * Withdraws the specified amount from the user's account.
 *
 * @param accountId The account ID.
 * @param amount    The amount to withdraw (must be positive).
 * @throws InsufficientFundsException if the account balance is insufficient.
 * @throws IllegalArgumentException if the amount is non-positive.
 */
public void withdrawAmount(String accountId, double amount) {
    // Implementation details...
}
```

4. Consider Unexported Fields

- **Include Relevant Fields:**
    - When documenting a class, consider unexported (non-public) fields as well.
    - Explain their purpose and any constraints associated with them.

Example (Class with Unexported Field):

```
/**
 * Represents an online shopping cart.
 *
 * @param items The list of items in the cart.
 */
public class ShoppingCart {
    private List<Item> items;

    // Implementation details...
}
```

Remember, well-crafted doc comments contribute to code clarity, maintainability, and collaboration. By following these best practices, you enhance the overall quality of your Java codebase.

- **Effective Strategies for Minimizing Local Variable Scope in Java**

In the world of software development, writing clean, maintainable code is paramount. One often overlooked aspect of code quality is the **scope of local variables**. In Java, local variables are declared within a method, constructor, or block of code and have limited visibility. In this article, we'll explore effective strategies for minimizing local variable scope, leading to more readable and maintainable code.

Why Minimize Local Variable Scope?

1. Readability

Keeping variable scope as narrow as possible enhances code readability. When a variable's scope is limited to the smallest necessary context, it becomes easier to understand its purpose. Developers can quickly identify where a variable is used and reason about its behavior.

2. Maintainability

Code maintenance is a significant part of software development. By minimizing local variable scope, we reduce the cognitive load on future maintainers. When variables have a concise lifespan, it's simpler to track their state changes and troubleshoot issues.

Strategies for Minimizing Local Variable Scope

1. Declare Variables Where They're Used

One effective strategy is to declare variables close to their first usage. Avoid declaring variables at the beginning of a method unless they are genuinely needed there. By doing so, you reduce the need for excessive scrolling and searching when reading code.

Consider the following example:

```
public void processOrder(Order order) {
    // Unnecessary early declaration
    List<Item> items;

    if (order.isReadyForProcessing()) {
        // Declare items only where needed
        List<Item> readyItems = order.getItems();
        // Process readyItems...
    }
    // Other code...
}
```

2. Initializer Best Practices

Include initializers in local variable declarations whenever possible. Initializing variables at the point of declaration improves code clarity. For instance:

```java
public void calculateTotalPrice(Order order) {
    double totalPrice = 0.0; // Initialize here
    for (Item item : order.getItems()) {
        totalPrice += item.getPrice();
    }
    // Use totalPrice...
}
```

3. Loops and Variable Scope

Loops provide an excellent opportunity to minimize variable scope. Declare loop-related variables within the loop itself. This practice avoids unintentional reuse of loop variables outside their intended context.

```java
public void printEvenNumbers(int[] numbers) {
    for (int num : numbers) {
        if (num % 2 == 0) {
            // num is only needed within this block
            System.out.println("Even number: " + num);
        }
    }
}
```

4. Method Size and Variable Scope

The size of a method correlates with local variable scope. Large methods tend to have broader variable visibility, making it harder to track variable lifetimes. Consider breaking down large methods into smaller, focused ones. Each method should have a clear purpose and minimal variable overlap.

Minimizing local variable scope in Java is a simple yet powerful technique. By following these strategies, you'll write cleaner, more maintainable code. Remember that readability and maintainability are essential for long-term project success.

Let's dive deeper into the topic of declaring variables where they're used and how it improves code readability and maintainability.

Declare Variables Where They're Used

The Problem

When writing code, it's common to declare variables at the beginning of a method or block. However, this practice can lead to unnecessarily broad variable scope. Consider the following example:

```java
public void processOrder(Order order) {
    // Unnecessary early declaration
    List<Item> items;

    if (order.isReadyForProcessing()) {
        // Declare items only where needed
        List<Item> readyItems = order.getItems();
        // Process readyItems...
```

```
    }
  // Other code...
}
```

In this snippet, the variable items is declared at the start of the method, even though it's only used within the if block. As a result, developers reading this code must scroll up and down to understand its context.

The Solution

To minimize local variable scope, declare variables as close to their first usage as possible. Here's the improved version of the previous example:

```
public void processOrder(Order order) {
  if (order.isReadyForProcessing()) {
    // Declare items only where needed
    List<Item> readyItems = order.getItems();
    // Process readyItems...
  }
  // Other code...
}
```

By doing this, we achieve several benefits:

1. **Readability**: Developers can quickly identify where a variable is used and understand its purpose. There's no need to search through lengthy code sections.

2. **Maintainability**: Future maintainers won't need to keep track of unnecessary variables. The scope is limited to the relevant context, making troubleshooting and debugging easier.

Best Practices

- **Avoid Early Declarations**: Only declare variables when they are genuinely needed. If a variable is used within a specific block, declare it there.

- **Think Locally**: Consider the smallest context in which a variable is required. Declare it within that context to keep the scope narrow.

- **Be Explicit**: Name your variables descriptively. Clear names help others understand their purpose even when the scope is limited.

Remember, minimizing local variable scope contributes to cleaner, more efficient code.

Initializer Best Practices in Java

When writing Java code, including initializers in local variable declarations is a powerful practice that enhances code clarity and improves understanding. Let's explore why this approach is beneficial and how it impacts code behavior.

What Are Initializers?

An initializer is an expression or value assigned to a variable at the point of declaration. It ensures that the variable starts with a specific value, even before any explicit assignment occurs. In the context of local variables, initializers play a crucial role in making code more concise and self-explanatory.

Benefits of Including Initializers

1. Clear Intent

When you initialize a variable right where it's declared, you communicate its purpose explicitly. Other developers reading your code immediately understand the initial state of the variable. For example:

```java
public void calculateTotalPrice(Order order) {
    double totalPrice = 0.0; // Initialize here
    for (Item item : order.getItems()) {
        totalPrice += item.getPrice();
    }
    // Use totalPrice...
}
```

In this snippet, totalPrice starts at zero, and its purpose is evident. Without the initializer, someone reviewing the code might wonder whether it was accidentally left uninitialized.

2. Behavior Prediction

Including initializers aids in predicting variable behavior. When you see an initialized variable, you know its starting value. This knowledge helps reason about subsequent operations. For instance:

```java
public void processOrder(Order order) {
    boolean readyForProcessing = order.isReadyForProcessing(); // Initialize here
    if (readyForProcessing) {
        // Process the order...
    }
    // Other code...
}
```

By initializing readyForProcessing, we anticipate its value within the if block. It simplifies mental tracking and reduces surprises.

3. Avoiding Default Values

Java assigns default values to variables (e.g., 0 for int, false for boolean). However, relying on these defaults can lead to subtle bugs. Explicit initializers prevent accidental reliance on default values.

153

Best Practices

1. **Initialize at Declaration**: Whenever possible, provide an initial value when declaring a local variable. Be explicit about the starting state.

2. **Avoid Deferred Initialization**: Delaying initialization until later in the method can confuse readers. Initialize variables where they are logically needed.

3. **Be Consistent**: Apply this practice consistently throughout your codebase. Consistency improves maintainability.

By including initializers in local variable declarations, you create self-documenting code. Your intentions are clear, and future maintainers will appreciate the predictability. Remember: clarity and predictability lead to robust software.

Loops and Variable Scope in Java

In Java, loops present a unique opportunity to **minimize the scope of variables**. By understanding how variable scope works within loops, we can write cleaner and more efficient code. Let's delve into this topic and compare for loops with while loops.

Variable Scope Basics

Before we dive into loops, let's recap variable scope:

- **Local Variables**: These are declared within methods, constructors, or blocks. Their scope is limited to the specific context where they are defined.

Minimizing Variable Scope with Loops

1. Declare Loop Indices Within the Loop

Consider the following example using a for loop:

```java
public class ScopeExample {
    public static void main(String[] args) {
        for (int i = 0; i < 10; i++) {
            // Contains declaration
            // Do operations...
        }
    }
}
```

In this snippet, the variable i is declared directly within the for loop. Its scope is restricted to the loop block. Once the loop ends, i ceases to exist.

2. Benefits of Declaring Within the Loop

- **Readability**: When the declaration is close to the initialization, the code becomes easier to read. Developers can quickly understand the purpose of the loop variable.
- **Documentation**: Declaring within the loop better documents how the variable is used. It's a clear signal that i is specific to this loop iteration.

3. Comparing for Loops and while Loops

- **for Loops**: These are ideal for minimizing variable scope. The initialization, condition, and update are all concise and contained within the loop header.
- **while Loops**: While loops can also be used, but they require separate declarations outside the loop. This can lead to broader variable scope if not managed carefully.

Method Size and Variable Scope in Java

In the world of software development, **method size** and **variable scope** play crucial roles in writing maintainable and efficient code. Let's explore their relationship and discuss strategies for improving code organization.

The Importance of Method Size

Large methods can become unwieldy and challenging to understand. As a developer, you've likely encountered lengthy methods that try to do too much. Here's why method size matters:

1. **Readability**: Smaller methods are easier to read and comprehend. When a method focuses on a specific task, its purpose becomes clearer.
2. **Maintainability**: Large methods are harder to maintain. Changes or bug fixes can inadvertently impact unrelated parts of the code. Smaller methods reduce the risk of unintended side effects.

Local Variable Scope

In Java, local variables are declared within methods or blocks. Their scope is limited to the specific context where they are defined. Let's explore the different types of local variables:

1. **Method Parameters**: These are supplied to a method when it's invoked.
2. **Local Variables Inside Methods**:
   - These variables are declared within a method and can't be accessed outside of it.
   - They don't exist after the method's execution is over.

Strategies for Improving Code Organization

1. Declare Variables Where Needed

- Follow the practice of declaring variables close to their first usage.
- Avoid early declarations at the beginning of a method unless genuinely needed.
- This reduces the need for excessive scrolling and searching when reading code.

2. Initializer Best Practices

- Include initializers in local variable declarations.
- Initializing variables at the point of declaration improves code clarity and behavior.

3. Loop Variables and Block Scope

- Declare loop-related variables within the loop itself.
- For example, use for loops with locally scoped indices.
- Avoid relying on variables declared outside the loop.

4. Break Down Large Methods

- If a method performs multiple distinct tasks, consider breaking it down into smaller, focused methods.
- Each method should have a clear purpose and minimal variable overlap.
- Smaller methods are easier to test, debug, and maintain.

Example: Predicting Output

Let's predict the output of the following Java program:

```java
public class Test {
  static int x = 11;
  private int y = 33;

  public void method1(int x) {
    Test t = new Test();
    this.x = 22;
    y = 44;
    System.out.println("Test.x: " + Test.x);
    System.out.println("t.x: " + t.x);
    System.out.println("t.y: " + t.y);
    System.out.println("y: " + y);
  }

  public static void main(String[] args) {
    Test t = new Test();
    t.method1(5);
  }
}
```

Output:

- Test.x: 22
- t.x: 22
- t.y: 33
- y: 44

Remember, well-organized code with appropriately scoped variables leads to more maintainable software.

- ## Advantages of For-Each Loops in Java: Simplifying Iteration

Introduction to Loops in Java

Loops play a crucial role in programming by allowing us to repeat a set of instructions multiple times. In Java, loops are essential for performing repetitive tasks, such as iterating over arrays, lists, or other collections. They help us process data efficiently and automate tasks that involve repetition.

In this article, we'll focus on one specific type of loop: the **for-each loop** (also known as the **enhanced for-loop**). We'll explore why for-each loops are often preferred over traditional for loops and discuss their advantages.

Traditional For Loops

Before diving into for-each loops, let's briefly revisit traditional for loops. The classic for loop has the following structure:

```
for (initialization; condition; update) {
    // Code to be executed in each iteration
}
```

Here's what each part of the traditional for loop means:

1. **Initialization**: This step initializes a loop control variable (usually an index) before the loop starts.
2. **Condition**: The loop continues executing as long as the condition evaluates to true.
3. **Update**: After each iteration, the update statement modifies the loop control variable.

Traditional for loops are powerful and flexible. They allow us to iterate over a range of values, such as array indices or a fixed number of iterations. However, they have some drawbacks:

- **Index Management**: We need to manage an explicit index variable, which can lead to off-by-one errors or other mistakes.
- **Readability**: The syntax can be verbose, especially when dealing with complex data structures.
- **Modifying Lists**: Traditional loops allow modifying the list during iteration, which can be risky.

For-Each Loops (Enhanced For-Loop)

The for-each loop was introduced in Java 5 to simplify iteration. Its syntax is more concise and readable:

```
for (ElementType element : collection) {
    // Code to be executed for each element
}
```

Here's what each part of the for-each loop means:

1. **ElementType**: The data type of the elements in the collection.
2. **element**: A temporary variable that represents each element in the collection.
3. **collection**: The iterable collection (e.g., an array, a list, or a set).

Advantages of for-each loops:

1. **Readability**: For-each loops enhance code readability. We don't need to manage an index, making the code cleaner and easier to understand.
2. **No Index Errors**: Since there's no explicit index, we avoid common index-related mistakes.
3. **Efficient Iteration**: For-each loops internally use an iterator, making them efficient for most collections.
4. **Applicable to Any Iterable**: Unlike traditional loops, for-each works with any iterable collection, not just lists.

However, there's one important caveat:

- **Immutable Collection**: For-each loops do not allow modifying the collection during iteration. Attempting to do so may result in a ConcurrentModificationException.

When to Use Each Type of Loop

1. **Use For-Each Loops By Default**:

   - Whenever possible, prefer for-each loops for their readability and simplicity.
   - Use them for read-only operations where modification isn't required.

2. **Exceptions for Traditional Loops**:

   - Use traditional loops when you need an explicit index (e.g., accessing adjacent elements).
   - When modifying the list during iteration is necessary (though it's generally discouraged).

In summary, for-each loops simplify iteration, improve code quality, and are the go-to choice for most scenarios. However, choose the right loop based on your specific requirements.

Let's delve into the details of **traditional for loops** in Java:

Traditional For Loops

A traditional for loop in Java has the following structure:

```
for (initialization; condition; update) {
    // Code to be executed in each iteration
}
```

Here's what each part of the traditional for loop means:

1. **Initialization**: This step initializes a loop control variable (usually an index) before the loop starts. For example:

   ```
   for (int i = 0; i < array.length; i++) {
       // Code here
   }
   ```

   - The variable i is initialized to 0.
   - The loop continues as long as i is less than the length of the array.
   - After each iteration, i is incremented.

2. **Condition**: The loop continues executing as long as the condition evaluates to true. In the example above, the condition is i < array.length.

3. **Update**: After each iteration, the update statement modifies the loop control variable. In our example, i is incremented (i++).

Advantages and Considerations

Traditional loops have their strengths and limitations:

- **Index Management**: We explicitly manage an index variable (i in our example). While this allows precise control over the iteration, it can lead to off-by-one errors or other mistakes.

- **Modification During Iteration**: Traditional loops allow modifying the list during iteration. However, this flexibility can be risky. If we add or remove elements from the list, we need to adjust the index accordingly.

- **Efficiency with RandomAccess Lists**: Traditional loops work efficiently with **RandomAccess** lists (like ArrayList). Since these lists provide direct access to elements by index, the loop performs well.

- **Less Efficient with LinkedList**: On the other hand, traditional loops are less efficient when used with **LinkedLists**. Accessing elements by index in a linked list involves traversing the list, which can be slower.

In summary, traditional for loops are powerful and flexible, but they require careful management of indices and consideration of list modifications. When efficiency matters, choose the appropriate list type based on your use case.

Remember, the choice between traditional loops and for-each loops depends on readability, performance, and specific requirements.

For-Each Loops (Enhanced For-Loop)

The **for-each loop**, also known as the **enhanced for-loop**, is a powerful construct introduced in Java to simplify iteration over collections. Let's explore its features and advantages:

1. **Syntax**:

    - The for-each loop has a concise syntax:

    ```
    for (ElementType element : collection) {
        // Code to be executed for each element
    }
    ```

        - ElementType represents the data type of the elements in the collection.
        - element is a temporary variable that holds each element during iteration.
        - collection refers to the iterable collection (e.g., an array, a list, or a set).

2. **Eliminating the Explicit Index**:

    - One of the most significant benefits of for-each loops is that they eliminate the need for an explicit index variable.
    - Without managing an index, the code becomes cleaner and more readable.
    - We focus solely on processing each element, rather than juggling indices.

3. **Readability and Cleaner Code**:

    - For-each loops enhance code readability by abstracting away the low-level details.
    - Developers can express their intent directly, making the code more intuitive.
    - The loop's purpose is evident: "For each element in the collection, do something."

4. **Applicable to Any Collection**:

    - Unlike traditional loops, for-each loops work with any iterable collection, not just lists.
    - Whether it's an array, an ArrayList, a HashSet, or any other iterable, the for-each loop adapts seamlessly.
    - It internally uses an iterator to traverse the collection.

5. **ConcurrentModificationException**:

    - While for-each loops simplify iteration, they come with a limitation.
    - Attempting to modify the collection during iteration (e.g., adding or removing elements) may lead to a ConcurrentModificationException.
    - To avoid this, ensure that modifications occur outside the loop.

For-each loops provide a cleaner syntax, better readability, and compatibility with various collections. Use them by default for read-only operations. When you need an explicit index or plan to modify the collection, consider traditional loops.

When to Use Each Type of Loop: Making the Right Choice

Choosing between traditional `for` loops and for-each loops (enhanced for-loops) depends on the specific requirements of your code. Let's explore scenarios where each type of loop shines:

- **For-Each Loops (Enhanced For-Loops)**

Use Cases:

- **Read-Only Iteration**:

  - **Recommendation**: By default, prefer for-each loops for their readability and simplicity.
  - **Why?**: For-each loops abstract away the index management, resulting in cleaner code.
  - **Examples**:

    ```
    List<String> names = Arrays.asList("Alice", "Bob", "Charlie");
    for (String name : names) {
        System.out.println(name);
    }
    ```

- **Collections and Iterables**:

  - **Recommendation**: Use for-each loops when iterating over any iterable collection (not just lists).
  - **Why?**: For-each works seamlessly with arrays, lists, sets, maps, and custom iterable classes.
  - **Examples**:

    ```
    Set<Integer> numbers = new HashSet<>(Arrays.asList(1, 2, 3));
    for (int num : numbers) {
        System.out.println(num);
    }
    ```

Limitations:

- **No Index Access**:
  - For-each loops do not provide direct access to indices.
  - Use them when you don't need to modify the collection during iteration.

2. Traditional Loops

Use Cases:

- **Explicit Index Required**:

  - **Recommendation**: Use traditional loops when you need an explicit index (e.g., accessing adjacent elements).
  - **Why?**: Traditional loops allow precise control over the iteration variable.
  - **Examples**:

    ```
    String[] fruits = {"Apple", "Banana", "Orange"};
    for (int i = 0; i < fruits.length; i++) {
        System.out.println("Fruit at index " + i + ": " + fruits[i]);
    }
    ```

- **Modifying the List During Iteration**:
  - **Recommendation**: Although discouraged, traditional loops allow modifying the list during iteration.
  - **Why?**: Sometimes you need to add, remove, or update elements within the loop.
  - **Examples**:

```
List<Integer> numbers = new ArrayList<>(Arrays.asList(1, 2, 3));
for (int i = 0; i < numbers.size(); i++) {
  if (numbers.get(i) % 2 == 0) {
    numbers.remove(i);
  }
}
```

Considerations:

- **Efficiency with RandomAccess Lists**:
  - Traditional loops work efficiently with **RandomAccess** lists (e.g., ArrayList).
  - For linked lists, consider other options due to traversal overhead.

In summary, choose the right loop based on your specific needs. Prioritize readability with for-each loops, but be aware of their limitations. Traditional loops remain valuable when explicit indices or list modifications are necessary.

Traditional For Loops in Java

A **traditional for loop** is a fundamental construct in Java for iterating over a range of values. Let's break down its structure and explore its characteristics:

Structure of a Traditional For Loop

The classic for loop has the following components:

1. **Initialization**: In this step, we initialize a loop control variable (usually an index) before the loop begins. For example:

```
for (int i = 0; i < array.length; i++) {
  // Code executed in each iteration
}
```

   - The variable i is initialized to 0.
   - The loop continues as long as the condition i < array.length holds true.
   - After each iteration, i is incremented.
2. **Condition**: The loop executes as long as the specified condition evaluates to true. In our example, the condition is i < array.length.

3. **Update**: After each iteration, the update statement modifies the loop control variable (i++ in our example).

Advantages and Considerations

Traditional loops offer flexibility but come with certain considerations:

1. **Index Management**:

    - We explicitly manage an index variable (i in our example).
    - While this allows precise control over the iteration, it can lead to off-by-one errors or other mistakes.

2. **Modification During Iteration**:

    - Traditional loops allow modifying the list during iteration.
    - However, this flexibility can be risky. If we add or remove elements from the list, we need to adjust the index accordingly.

3. **Efficiency with RandomAccess Lists**:

    - Traditional loops work efficiently with **RandomAccess** lists (e.g., ArrayList).
    - Since these lists provide direct access to elements by index, the loop performs well.

4. **Less Efficient with LinkedList**:

    - When used with **LinkedLists**, traditional loops are less efficient.
    - Accessing elements by index in a linked list involves traversal, which can be slower.

In summary, traditional for loops are powerful but require careful management of indices and consideration of list modifications. Choose the appropriate list type based on your specific use case.

Remember, the choice between traditional loops and for-each loops depends on readability, performance, and specific requirements.

For-Each Loops (Enhanced For-Loop)

The **for-each loop**, also known as the **enhanced for-loop**, is a powerful construct introduced in Java to simplify iteration over collections. Let's explore its features and advantages:

1. **Syntax**:

    - The for-each loop has a concise syntax:

    ```
    for (ElementType element : collection) {
        // Code to be executed for each element
    }
    ```

        - ElementType represents the data type of the elements in the collection.
        - element is a temporary variable that holds each element during iteration.
        - collection refers to the iterable collection (e.g., an array, a list, or a set).

2. **Eliminating the Explicit Index**:

- One of the most significant benefits of for-each loops is that they eliminate the need for an explicit index variable.
- Without managing an index, the code becomes cleaner and more readable.
- We focus solely on processing each element, rather than juggling indices.

3. **Readability and Cleaner Code**:

- For-each loops enhance code readability by abstracting away the low-level details.
- Developers can express their intent directly, making the code more intuitive.
- The loop's purpose is evident: "For each element in the collection, do something."

4. **Applicable to Any Collection**:

- Unlike traditional loops, for-each loops work with any iterable collection, not just lists.
- Whether it's an array, an ArrayList, a HashSet, or any other iterable, the for-each loop adapts seamlessly.
- It internally uses an iterator to traverse the collection.

5. **ConcurrentModificationException**:

- While for-each loops simplify iteration, they come with a limitation.
- Attempting to modify the collection during iteration (e.g., adding or removing elements) may lead to a ConcurrentModificationException.

In summary, for-each loops provide a cleaner syntax, better readability, and compatibility with various collections. Use them by default for read-only operations. When you need an explicit index or plan to modify the collection, consider traditional loops.

When to Use Each Type of Loop: Making the Right Choice

Choosing between traditional for loops and for-each loops (enhanced for-loops) depends on the specific requirements of your code. Let's explore scenarios where each type of loop shines:

1. For-Each Loops (Enhanced For-Loops)

Use Cases:

- **Read-Only Iteration**:

  - **Recommendation**: By default, prefer for-each loops for their readability and simplicity.
  - **Why?**: For-each loops abstract away the index management, resulting in cleaner code.
  - **Examples**:

    ```
    List<String> names = Arrays.asList("Alice", "Bob", "Charlie");
    for (String name : names) {
        System.out.println(name);
    }
    ```

- **Collections and Iterables**:
    - **Recommendation**: Use for-each loops when iterating over any iterable collection (not just lists).
    - **Why?**: For-each works seamlessly with arrays, lists, sets, maps, and custom iterable classes.
    - **Examples**:

```
Set<Integer> numbers = new HashSet<>(Arrays.asList(1, 2, 3));
for (int num : numbers) {
    System.out.println(num);
}
```

Limitations:

- **No Index Access**:
    - For-each loops do not provide direct access to indices.
    - Use them when you don't need to modify the collection during iteration.

2. Traditional Loops

Use Cases:

- **Explicit Index Required**:

    - **Recommendation**: Use traditional loops when you need an explicit index (e.g., accessing adjacent elements).
    - **Why?**: Traditional loops allow precise control over the iteration variable.
    - **Examples**:

```
String[] fruits = {"Apple", "Banana", "Orange"};
for (int i = 0; i < fruits.length; i++) {
    System.out.println("Fruit at index " + i + ": " + fruits[i]);
}
```

- **Modifying the List During Iteration**:

    - **Recommendation**: Although discouraged, traditional loops allow modifying the list during iteration.
    - **Why?**: Sometimes you need to add, remove, or update elements within the loop.
    - **Examples**:

```
List<Integer> numbers = new ArrayList<>(Arrays.asList(1, 2, 3));
for (int i = 0; i < numbers.size(); i++) {
    if (numbers.get(i) % 2 == 0) {
        numbers.remove(i);
    }
}
```

167

Considerations:

- **Efficiency with RandomAccess Lists**:
  - Traditional loops work efficiently with **RandomAccess** lists (e.g., ArrayList).
  - For linked lists, consider other options due to traversal overhead.

In summary, choose the right loop based on your specific needs. Prioritize readability with for-each loops, but be aware of their limitations. Traditional loops remain valuable when explicit indices or list modifications are necessary.

• Mastering Java Libraries

Java libraries play a pivotal role in modern software development. They empower developers by providing pre-built, reusable components that enhance productivity, maintainability, and code quality. In this comprehensive guide, we'll delve into the world of Java libraries, exploring their significance, popular choices, and best practices for effective utilization.

1. Understanding Java Libraries

What Are Libraries in Java?

Libraries, also known as packages or modules, are collections of classes, interfaces, and resources bundled together to serve a specific purpose. They encapsulate functionality, making it accessible to other parts of your application. Java's extensive library ecosystem covers a wide range of domains, from data manipulation to web services.

Why Use Libraries?

- **Code Reusability**: Libraries save time and effort by providing pre-implemented solutions. Rather than reinventing the wheel, developers can leverage existing code.
- **Quality Assurance**: Established libraries undergo rigorous testing and maintenance, reducing the risk of bugs and security vulnerabilities.
- **Focus on Business Logic**: By relying on libraries, developers can concentrate on solving domain-specific problems rather than low-level details.

2. Popular Java Libraries and Their Purposes

Apache Commons

- **Purpose**: Apache Commons offers a collection of reusable components, including utilities for string manipulation, file I/O, and data structures.
- **Key Components**:
  - StringUtils: Handy methods for string handling.
  - IOUtils: Simplified I/O operations.
  - Collections: Additional data structures (e.g., ListUtils, MapUtils).

Google Guava

- **Purpose**: Google Guava enhances core Java functionalities, providing elegant solutions for common programming tasks.
- **Features**:
  - Functional programming utilities.
  - Immutable collections.
  - Precondition checks.

- Graph libraries.

Jackson

- **Purpose**: Jackson is a powerful library for working with JSON data.
- **Features**:
    - JSON serialization and deserialization.
    - Streaming API for efficient processing.
    - Support for custom serializers/deserializers.

Log4j

- **Purpose**: Log4j simplifies logging and debugging.
- **Benefits**:
    - Configurable logging levels.
    - Appender architecture (console, file, database).
    - Log rotation and rolling files.

JUnit

- **Purpose**: JUnit is the go-to library for unit testing in Java.
- **Features**:
    - Annotations for test methods (@Test).
    - Assertions (assertEquals, assertTrue, etc.).
    - Test suites and parameterized tests.

3. Creating Custom Libraries

Building Your Own Java Library

- Identify a specific need or functionality.
- Design your library's API (classes, methods, interfaces).
- Implement the core logic.
- Package your library (JAR, Maven, Gradle).

Packaging and Distributing Your Library

- Use build tools (Maven, Gradle) to create distributable artifacts.
- Publish your library to a repository (e.g., Maven Central).
- Document your library's usage and API.

Remember, mastering Java libraries involves not only using existing ones but also creating your own when necessary. Choose wisely, keep dependencies minimal, and explore the vast Java ecosystem.

Let's delve into some common Java libraries and explore their features:

1. Apache Commons

Purpose: Apache Commons provides a collection of reusable components that simplify various programming tasks. Here are some key components:

- **StringUtils**: A utility class for string manipulation. It offers methods for handling strings efficiently.
- **IOUtils**: Simplifies input/output operations, making file handling easier.
- **Collections**: Additional data structures beyond Java's standard library (e.g., ListUtils, MapUtils).

2. Google Guava

Purpose: Google Guava enhances core Java functionalities by providing elegant solutions. Some notable features include:

- **Functional Programming Utilities**: Guava offers functional programming utilities, making code concise and expressive.
- **Immutable Collections**: Immutable lists, sets, and maps for safer data handling.
- **Precondition Checks**: Convenient methods for validating preconditions.
- **Graph Libraries**: Tools for working with graphs and networks.

3. Jackson

Purpose: Jackson is a powerful library for working with JSON data. Its features include:

- **JSON Serialization and Deserialization**: Easily convert Java objects to JSON and vice versa.
- **Streaming API**: Efficiently process large JSON data streams.
- **Custom Serializers/Deserializers**: Customize how objects are converted to JSON and back.

4. Log4j

Purpose: Log4j simplifies logging and debugging in Java applications. Its benefits include:

- **Configurable Logging Levels**: Control the verbosity of log messages (e.g., debug, info, error).
- **Appender Architecture**: Choose where log messages go (console, file, database).
- **Log Rotation and Rolling Files**: Manage log files effectively.

5. JUnit

Purpose: JUnit is the de facto standard for unit testing in Java. Its features include:

- **Annotations for Test Methods**: Use @Test to mark test methods.
- **Assertions**: Convenient methods like assertEquals, assertTrue, etc.
- **Test Suites and Parameterized Tests**: Organize and parameterize your tests.

Remember to explore these libraries further and choose wisely based on your project's requirements.

Let's explore the process of creating custom libraries in Java:

1. Building Your Own Java Library

Creating a custom Java library involves several steps. Here's a guide to get you started:

Identify a Specific Need or Functionality

Before diving into implementation, identify the purpose of your library. What problem does it solve? Consider areas where existing libraries fall short or where you need specialized functionality.

Design Your Library's API

- Define the classes, methods, and interfaces that your library will expose.
- Keep the API clean, intuitive, and consistent. Think about how developers will interact with your library.

Implement the Core Logic

Write the actual code for your library. This includes:

- Implementing the desired functionality.
- Handling edge cases and error scenarios.
- Ensuring good performance and efficiency.

Package Your Library

- Choose a packaging format (e.g., JAR, Maven, Gradle).
- Organize your code into packages and directories.
- Include any necessary resources (configuration files, documentation).

2. Packaging and Distributing Your Library

Use Build Tools

- **Maven**: If you're using Maven, create a pom.xml file that specifies your library's dependencies, version, and other relevant information.
- **Gradle**: For Gradle, define your library in the build.gradle file.

Create Distributable Artifacts

- Build your library using the chosen build tool. This generates a distributable artifact (e.g., JAR file).
- Ensure that the artifact contains all necessary classes and resources.

Publish Your Library

- If you want others to use your library, consider publishing it to a repository (e.g., Maven Central).
- Follow the repository's guidelines for uploading your artifact.

3. Documenting APIs for Others to Use

- Write clear and concise documentation for your library's API.
- Include usage examples, explanations of classes and methods, and any relevant notes.
- Consider generating Javadoc comments for automatic documentation.

Remember that creating a custom library is both a technical and user-focused endeavor. Strive for simplicity, maintainability, and usefulness.

- ## Avoid Float and Double

Introduction

When it comes to handling numbers with decimal points, programmers often turn to the float and double primitive types. These types allow for the representation of approximate floating-point values across a wide range of magnitudes. However, it's essential to understand that both float and double are **approximations**. When precise answers are crucial—especially in scenarios like financial calculations or other precise computations—it's advisable to steer clear of these types.

The Limitations of Floating-Point Types

1. **IEEE 754 Standard**: Java adheres to the IEEE 754 standard for representing floating-point numbers. Here's how it breaks down:
   - A float uses 32 bits, divided into:
     - 1 bit for the sign (positive or negative)
     - 8 bits for the exponent
     - 23 bits for the mantissa (fractional part)
   - Despite its limitations, this format can represent a wide range of values.
2. **Approximation**: Floating-point types sacrifice accuracy for versatility. As you move further from zero, the precision diminishes due to the inherent limitations of the data format.
3. **Example**: Consider the number 1.23. In IEEE 754 format, the sign denotes positivity, the mantissa represents 123, and the exponent corresponds to 10^{-2}.

Alternatives for Exact Numbers

1. **Use int or long**: When precision matters, opt for int or long and handle the decimal point manually. For instance, in simple calculations involving money, adding and subtracting from an integer value works well.
2. **BigDecimal**: For more complex scenarios, turn to BigDecimal. Although it sacrifices speed, it provides immense power. Keep in mind that interacting with BigDecimal may require additional effort compared to using primitive types.

Remember, when exact answers are crucial, prioritize precision over approximation. By avoiding the pitfalls of float and double, you can ensure accurate results in your Java programs!

Let's delve into the topic of avoiding float and double in Java when precise answers are required.

When dealing with numbers that include a decimal point, programmers often reach for either float or double. These primitive types facilitate the representation of approximate floating-point values over various magnitudes. However, it's crucial to recognize that these types are **approximations**. If you need exact answers—especially when dealing with financial calculations or other precise computations —you should avoid using float and double.

The Limitations of Floating-Point Types

1. **IEEE 754 Standard**: Java implements the IEEE 754 standard for representing floating-point numbers. A float uses 32 bits, divided into 1 bit for the sign, 8 bits for the exponent, and 23 bits for the mantissa. Despite its limitations, this format can represent a wide range of values.
2. **Approximation**: Floating-point types sacrifice accuracy for versatility. As you move further from zero, the accuracy drops due to the limitations of the data format.
3. **Example**: For the number 1.23, the sign denotes positivity, the mantissa represents 123, and the exponent corresponds to 10^{-2}.

Alternatives for Exact Numbers

1. **Use int or long**: When precision matters, consider using int or long and handle the decimal point manually. For instance, in simple calculations involving money, adding and subtracting from an integer value works well.
2. **BigDecimal**: For more complex scenarios, employ BigDecimal. Although it sacrifices speed, it provides immense power. Be aware that interacting with BigDecimal may require additional effort compared to primitive types.

Remember, when exact answers are crucial, choose precision over approximation. Avoid the pitfalls of float and double to ensure accurate results in your Java programs!

Certainly! Let's explore the alternatives to float and double when precise numbers are essential in Java:

Alternatives for Exact Numbers

1. Use int or long

- When precision matters, consider using int or long data types.
- Handle the decimal point manually by scaling the values appropriately.
- For example, in simple calculations involving money, adding and subtracting from an integer value works well.
- These integral types provide exact results without the approximation inherent in floating-point types.

2. BigDecimal

- For more complex scenarios, turn to BigDecimal.
- Although it sacrifices speed due to its object-oriented nature, it provides immense power.
- BigDecimal allows arbitrary precision arithmetic, making it suitable for financial calculations, scientific computations, and other situations where accuracy is paramount.
- Be aware that interacting with BigDecimal may require additional effort compared to using primitive types.

Remember, choosing the right data type depends on the specific requirements of your application. Prioritize precision over approximation when exact answers are crucial!

- ## Optimizing Performance: Choosing Primitives Over Boxed Primitives

Introduction

When writing Java code, developers often encounter a choice between using primitive data types or their boxed counterparts. While both serve similar purposes, understanding the differences and knowing when to prefer one over the other can significantly impact performance. In this article, we delve into the world of primitives and boxed primitives, exploring their characteristics and best practices.

1. Primitives vs. Boxed Primitives

1.1 Primitive Data Types

Primitive data types are the building blocks of Java. They represent simple values and are directly supported by the language. Here are some common primitive data types:

- **int**: Represents integer values (e.g., 42, -10).
- **double**: Represents floating-point numbers (e.g., 3.14, -0.5).
- **boolean**: Represents true or false values.
- And more: byte, short, long, float, char.

Characteristics of primitives:

- **Efficiency**: Primitives are memory-efficient and perform better due to their direct representation in memory.
- **No Null Value**: Primitives cannot be null.

1.2 Boxed Primitives

Boxed primitives, on the other hand, are objects that wrap primitive values. They belong to classes like Integer, Double, and Boolean. Here's why they exist:

- **Object-Oriented Context**: Java often requires objects (e.g., for collections, generics, and method overloading).
- **Nullable Values**: Boxed primitives can hold null values.

However, using boxed primitives introduces overhead:

- **Memory Overhead**: Each boxed object carries additional memory overhead (e.g., object header, reference).
- **Auto-Boxing and Unboxing**: Converting between primitives and boxed primitives incurs performance costs.

2. Performance Considerations

2.1 Memory Efficiency

When memory is critical (e.g., large datasets, mobile apps), primitives shine. They consume less memory, as they don't need the extra baggage of an object. For example:

```
int score = 100; // Primitive
Integer boxedScore = 100; // Boxed primitive
```

The memory footprint of score is smaller than that of boxedScore.

2.2 Auto-Boxing and Unboxing

Auto-boxing automatically converts primitives to boxed primitives and vice versa. While convenient, it comes at a cost:

```
List<Integer> numbers = new ArrayList<>();
numbers.add(42); // Auto-boxing
int retrievedValue = numbers.get(0); // Auto-unboxing
```

These implicit conversions impact performance, especially in tight loops or high-frequency operations.

3. Best Practices

3.1 When to Use Primitives

- **Arithmetic Operations**: Prefer primitives for arithmetic calculations.
- **Collections**: Use primitives for arrays and collections (e.g., int[], ArrayList<int>).
- **Performance-Critical Code**: Opt for primitives in performance-critical sections.

3.2 When to Use Boxed Primitives

- **Nullable Values**: When null is a valid state (e.g., database queries).
- **Generics**: Boxed primitives work well with generic types.
- **APIs Requiring Objects**: Some APIs expect objects (e.g., Java libraries).

Choosing between primitives and boxed primitives involves trade-offs. Prioritize performance by understanding the context and making informed decisions. By favoring primitives where possible, you'll write more efficient Java code. Remember: sometimes, less is more!

Performance Considerations: Primitives vs. Boxed Primitives in Java

When it comes to optimizing performance in Java, the choice between using **primitives** and their **boxed counterparts** (such as Integer, Double, and Boolean) is crucial. Let's explore the performance considerations associated with this decision.

Efficiency: Primitives vs. Boxed Primitives

1.1 Memory Efficiency

- **Primitives**: These fundamental data types (e.g., int, double, boolean) are memory-efficient. They directly represent values in memory without any additional overhead.
- **Boxed Primitives**: Boxed objects (e.g., Integer, Double) wrap primitive values but come with extra memory overhead (object headers, references).

Example:

```
int score = 100; // Primitive
Integer boxedScore = 100; // Boxed primitive
```

The memory footprint of score is smaller than that of boxedScore.

1.2 Auto-Boxing and Unboxing

Auto-boxing automatically converts between primitives and boxed primitives. While convenient, it impacts performance:

```
List<Integer> numbers = new ArrayList<>();
numbers.add(42); // Auto-boxing
int retrievedValue = numbers.get(0); // Auto-unboxing
```

These implicit conversions introduce overhead, especially in tight loops or frequent operations.

2. Overhead Associated with Boxed Primitives

2.1 Object Creation

- **Boxed Primitives**: Creating boxed objects involves memory allocation and object initialization.
- **Primitives**: No such overhead; they are ready for use.

2.2 Garbage Collection

- **Boxed Primitives**: When boxed objects go out of scope, they become eligible for garbage collection.
- **Primitives**: No garbage collection needed.

3. Impact on Performance

3.1 Performance Bottlenecks

- **Boxed Primitives**: In performance-critical scenarios, excessive use of boxed primitives can slow down your application.
- **Examples**: Frequent auto-boxing/unboxing, large collections of boxed objects.

3.2 Best Practices

- **Choose Primitives When Possible**:

    - Arithmetic operations: Use primitives for efficiency.
    - Collections (e.g., int[], ArrayList<int>): Prefer primitives.
    - Performance-critical code: Opt for primitives.

- **Use Boxed Primitives When Necessary**:

    - Nullable values (e.g., database queries).
    - Generics (where objects are required).
    - APIs expecting objects (e.g., Java libraries).

Understanding the trade-offs between primitives and boxed primitives empowers you to write more efficient Java code. By favoring primitives where appropriate, you'll enhance performance and keep your code lean. Remember: sometimes, less is more!

Auto-Boxing and Unboxing in Java

In Java, **auto-boxing** and **auto-unboxing** are features that simplify the interaction between primitive data types and their corresponding boxed counterparts. Let's explore these concepts and their impact on performance.

Understanding Auto-Boxing and Auto-Unboxing

1.1 Auto-Boxing

- **Auto-boxing** automatically converts a primitive value into its boxed equivalent.

- For example:

    int age = 30; // Primitive
    Integer ageBoxed = age; // Auto-boxing

    Here, age (a primitive int) is automatically converted to an Integer object.

1.2 Auto-Unboxing

- **Auto-unboxing** automatically extracts the primitive value from a boxed object.

- For example:

    Double priceBoxed = 99.99; // Boxed primitive
    double price = priceBoxed; // Auto-unboxing

    Here, priceBoxed (a boxed Double) is automatically converted to a primitive double.

2. Benefits and Considerations

2.1 Benefits of Auto-Boxing and Auto-Unboxing

- **Convenience**: Auto-boxing reduces verbosity by allowing seamless conversions.
- **Readability**: Code becomes more concise and expressive.

2.2 Performance Implications

- **Overhead**: Despite the convenience, auto-boxing introduces overhead:
    - **Memory**: Each boxed object consumes additional memory (object header, reference).
    - **Performance**: Implicit conversions impact performance, especially in loops or frequent operations.

3. Best Practices

- **Be Aware**: Understand when auto-boxing/unboxing occurs in your code.
- **Performance-Critical Sections**: Avoid excessive auto-boxing/unboxing in performance-critical areas.
- **Consider Primitives**: If memory and performance matter, prefer using primitives directly.

Auto-boxing and auto-unboxing strike a balance between convenience and performance. While they reduce verbosity, developers should be mindful of their impact. Choose wisely based on the context of your application!

Best Practices: Primitives vs. Boxed Primitives in Java

When it comes to optimizing performance in Java, understanding the trade-offs between **primitives** and their **boxed counterparts** (such as `Integer`, `Double`, and `Boolean`) is essential. Let's explore some best practices for making informed decisions.

When to Use Primitives

1.1 Arithmetic Operations

- **Prefer Primitives**: For arithmetic calculations (addition, subtraction, multiplication, etc.), use primitives.

- Example:

```
int total = 0;
for (int i = 1; i <= 100; i++) {
    total += i; // Efficient with primitives
}
```

1.2 Collections

- **Use Primitives for Arrays and Collections**:

    - Arrays: Prefer arrays of primitives (e.g., int[], double[]) over arrays of boxed primitives.
    - Collections (e.g., ArrayList<int>): Favor primitives.
- Example:

```
List<Integer> numbers = new ArrayList<>(); // Avoid if performance matters
int[] scores = new int[100]; // More memory-efficient
```

1.3 Performance-Critical Code

- **Opt for Primitives in Performance-Critical Sections**:
    - Loops, frequently executed methods, and time-sensitive operations benefit from using primitives.
    - Avoid unnecessary auto-boxing/unboxing.

2. When to Use Boxed Primitives

2.1 Nullable Values

- **Boxed Primitives for Nullable Values**:

    - When null is a valid state (e.g., database queries, optional parameters).
    - Boxed types allow representing absence of value.
- Example:

```
Integer nullableValue = getNullableValueFromDatabase();
if (nullableValue != null) {
   // Handle the value
}
```

2.2 Generics

- **Boxed Primitives Work Well with Generics**:

    - Generic classes and methods often require objects.
    - Use boxed primitives when working with generic types.
- Example:

```
List<Integer> genericList = new ArrayList<>();
// Works seamlessly with generics
```

2.3 APIs Requiring Objects

- **Some APIs Expect Objects**:

    - Java libraries or third-party APIs may require boxed primitives.

- Follow the API specifications.
- Example:

java.util.Collections.sort(listOfIntegers); // Requires List<Integer>

By following these best practices, you'll strike a balance between performance and flexibility. Remember that context matters, and thoughtful choices lead to efficient Java code.

• Prefer Other Types Over Strings in Java

When developing Java applications, selecting appropriate data types is crucial for efficient and maintainable code. While strings (String) are widely used, there are scenarios where other types offer better solutions. In this article, we'll delve into the reasons behind avoiding excessive use of strings and explore alternative data types.

1. Introduction to Primitives and Boxed Primitives

1.1 Primitive Data Types

Primitive data types are the fundamental building blocks in Java. They represent simple values and have specific characteristics:

- **int**: Represents integer values (e.g., 42, -10).
- **double**: Represents floating-point numbers (e.g., 3.14, -0.5).
- **boolean**: Represents true or false values.
- Other primitives include byte, short, long, float, and char.

Characteristics of primitives:

- **Efficiency**: Primitives are memory-efficient and perform better due to their direct representation in memory.
- **No Null Value**: Primitives cannot be null.

1.2 Boxed Primitives

Boxed primitives are objects that wrap primitive values. They belong to classes like Integer, Double, and Boolean. Reasons for their existence:

- **Object-Oriented Context**: Java often requires objects (e.g., for collections, generics, and method overloading).
- **Nullable Values**: Boxed primitives can hold null values.

However, using boxed primitives introduces overhead:

- **Memory Overhead**: Each boxed object carries additional memory overhead (e.g., object header, reference).
- **Auto-Boxing and Unboxing**: Converting between primitives and boxed primitives incurs performance costs.

2. Performance Considerations

2.1 Why Using Primitives Is More Efficient

- **Memory Efficiency**: Primitives consume less memory as they don't need the extra baggage of an object.

- Example:

```
int score = 100; // Primitive
Integer boxedScore = 100; // Boxed primitive
```

The memory footprint of score is smaller than that of boxedScore.

2.2 Overhead Associated with Boxed Primitives

- **Object Creation Overhead**:

  - Creating boxed objects involves memory allocation and object initialization.
  - Primitives are ready for use without such overhead.
- **Garbage Collection Overhead**:

  - Boxed objects become eligible for garbage collection when they go out of scope.
  - Primitives don't require garbage collection.

3. Best Practices

3.1 When to Use Primitives

- **Arithmetic Operations**: Prefer primitives for arithmetic calculations.
- **Collections**: Use primitives for arrays and collections (e.g., int[], ArrayList<int>).
- **Performance-Critical Code**: Opt for primitives in performance-critical sections.

3.2 When to Use Boxed Primitives

- **Nullable Values**: When null is a valid state (e.g., database queries).
- **Generics**: Boxed primitives work well with generic types.
- **APIs Requiring Objects**: Some APIs expect objects (e.g., Java libraries).

Choosing between primitives and boxed primitives involves trade-offs. Prioritize performance by understanding the context and making informed decisions. By favoring primitives where possible, you'll write more efficient Java code. Remember: sometimes, less is more!

Performance Considerations: Primitives vs. Boxed Primitives in Java

When optimizing performance in Java, understanding the trade-offs between **primitives** and their **boxed counterparts** (such as `Integer`, `Double`, and `Boolean`) is crucial. Let's explore why using primitives is generally more efficient and delve into the overhead associated with boxed primitives.

Efficiency: Primitives vs. Boxed Primitives

1.1 Memory Efficiency

- **Primitives**: These fundamental data types (e.g., int, double, boolean) are memory-efficient. They directly represent values in memory without any additional overhead.

- **Boxed Primitives**: Boxed objects (e.g., Integer, Double) wrap primitive values but come with extra memory overhead (object headers, references).

Example:

```
int score = 100; // Primitive
Integer boxedScore = 100; // Boxed primitive
```

The memory footprint of score is smaller than that of boxedScore.

1.2 Auto-Boxing and Unboxing

Auto-boxing automatically converts between primitives and boxed primitives. While convenient, it impacts performance:

```
List<Integer> numbers = new ArrayList<>();
numbers.add(42); // Auto-boxing
int retrievedValue = numbers.get(0); // Auto-unboxing
```

These implicit conversions introduce overhead, especially in tight loops or frequent operations.

2. Overhead Associated with Boxed Primitives

2.1 Object Creation Overhead

- **Boxed Primitives**: Creating boxed objects involves memory allocation and object initialization.
- **Primitives**: No such overhead; they are ready for use.

2.2 Garbage Collection Overhead

- **Boxed Primitives**: When boxed objects go out of scope, they become eligible for garbage collection.
- **Primitives**: No garbage collection needed.

3. Impact on Performance: Examples

3.1 Performance Bottlenecks

- **Boxed Primitives**: In performance-critical scenarios, excessive use of boxed primitives can slow down your application.
- **Examples**:
  - Frequent auto-boxing/unboxing in loops.
  - Large collections of boxed objects.

Understanding the balance between convenience and performance empowers you to make informed decisions. By favoring primitives where possible, you'll write more efficient Java code. Remember: sometimes, less is more!

Auto-Boxing and Unboxing in Java

In Java, **auto-boxing** and **auto-unboxing** are features that simplify the interaction between primitive data types and their corresponding boxed counterparts. Let's explore these concepts and their impact on performance.

1. Understanding Auto-Boxing and Auto-Unboxing

1.1 Auto-Boxing

- **Auto-boxing** automatically converts a primitive value into its boxed equivalent.

- For example:

```
int age = 30; // Primitive
Integer ageBoxed = age; // Auto-boxing
```

Here, age (a primitive int) is automatically converted to an Integer object.

1.2 Auto-Unboxing

- **Auto-unboxing** automatically extracts the primitive value from a boxed object.

- For example:

```
Double priceBoxed = 99.99; // Boxed primitive
double price = priceBoxed; // Auto-unboxing
```

Here, priceBoxed (a boxed Double) is automatically converted to a primitive double.

2. Benefits and Considerations

2.1 Benefits of Auto-Boxing and Auto-Unboxing

- **Convenience**: Auto-boxing reduces verbosity by allowing seamless conversions.
- **Readability**: Code becomes more concise and expressive.

2.2 Performance Implications

- **Overhead**: Despite the convenience, auto-boxing introduces overhead:
  - **Memory**: Each boxed object consumes additional memory (object header, reference).
  - **Performance**: Implicit conversions impact performance, especially in loops or frequent operations.

3. Best Practices

- **Be Aware**: Understand when auto-boxing/unboxing occurs in your code.

- **Performance-Critical Sections**: Avoid excessive auto-boxing/unboxing in performance-critical areas.
- **Consider Primitives**: If memory and performance matter, prefer using primitives directly.

Auto-boxing and auto-unboxing strike a balance between convenience and performance. While they reduce verbosity, developers should be mindful of their impact. Choose wisely based on the context of your application!

Best Practices: Primitives vs. Boxed Primitives in Java

When it comes to optimizing performance in Java, understanding the trade-offs between **primitives** and their **boxed counterparts** (such as `Integer`, `Double`, and `Boolean`) is essential. Let's explore some best practices for making informed decisions.

When to Use Primitives

1.1 Arithmetic Operations

- **Prefer Primitives**: For arithmetic calculations (addition, subtraction, multiplication, etc.), use primitives.

- Example:

```
int total = 0;
for (int i = 1; i <= 100; i++) {
    total += i; // Efficient with primitives
}
```

1.2 Collections

- **Use Primitives for Arrays and Collections**:

    - Arrays: Prefer arrays of primitives (e.g., int[], double[]) over arrays of boxed primitives.
    - Collections (e.g., ArrayList<int>): Favor primitives.
- Example:

```
List<Integer> numbers = new ArrayList<>(); // Avoid if performance matters
int[] scores = new int[100]; // More memory-efficient
```

1.3 Performance-Critical Code

- **Opt for Primitives in Performance-Critical Sections**:
    - Loops, frequently executed methods, and time-sensitive operations benefit from using primitives.
    - Avoid unnecessary auto-boxing/unboxing.

2. When to Use Boxed Primitives

2.1 Nullable Values

- **Boxed Primitives for Nullable Values**:

    - When null is a valid state (e.g., database queries).
    - Boxed types allow representing absence of value.
- Example:

```
Integer nullableValue = getNullableValueFromDatabase();
if (nullableValue != null) {
    // Handle the value
}
```

2.2 Generics

- **Boxed Primitives Work Well with Generics**:

    - Generic classes and methods often require objects.
    - Use boxed primitives when working with generic types.
- Example:

```
List<Integer> genericList = new ArrayList<>();
// Works seamlessly with generics
```

2.3 APIs Requiring Objects

- **Some APIs Expect Objects**:

    - Java libraries or third-party APIs may require boxed primitives.
    - Follow the API specifications.
- Example:

```
java.util.Collections.sort(listOfIntegers); // Requires List<Integer>
```

By following these best practices, you'll strike a balance between performance and flexibility. Remember that context matters, and thoughtful choices lead to efficient Java code.

- **Prefer Non-String Types When Appropriate**

In **Java**, it's essential to select appropriate data types for representing different kinds of information. While strings are versatile, they are not always the best choice. Let's explore scenarios where other types are more suitable:

1. **Primitive Types**: When dealing with numeric values, such as integers or floating-point numbers, prefer using primitive types like int, float, or double. These types offer better performance and memory efficiency compared to strings.

2. **Enum Types**: Enumerations represent a finite set of related constants. Instead of using strings to represent these, define an enum type. Enums provide type safety and make the code more expressive.

3. **Aggregate Types**: When combining multiple related values, avoid using strings as an aggregate. Instead, create a dedicated class to represent the aggregate. Consider using a private static member class for encapsulation.

```
// Inappropriate use of string as an aggregate type
String compoundKey = className + "#" + i.next();

// Better approach: Create a class to represent the aggregate
private static class CompoundKey {
    private final String className;
    private final String identifier;

    // Constructor, getters, and other methods...
}
```

4. **Capabilities (Unforgeable Keys)**: Strings are often misused as keys for thread-local variables. However, this approach can lead to shared global namespaces. Instead, use a dedicated key class to ensure uniqueness and type safety.

```
// Broken - inappropriate use of string as capability!
public class ThreadLocal {
    public static void set(String key, Object value);
    public static Object get(String key);
}

// Better approach: Use a key class
public class ThreadLocal {
    public static class Key {
        // Generates a unique, unforgeable key
    }

    public static Key getKey();
    public static void set(Key key, Object value);
    public static Object get(Key key);
}
```

Remember that strings can be cumbersome, less flexible, slower, and error-prone when used inappropriately. By choosing the right types, you'll write more robust and maintainable Java code.

• Optimizing String Concatenation in Java

In Java, string concatenation is a common operation when building strings dynamically. However, it's essential to understand the performance implications of different approaches. Let's delve into the key points related to string concatenation in Java.

Immutability of Strings

Strings in Java are **immutable**. Once a string is created, its value cannot be changed. When you concatenate two strings using the + operator, a new string is created, and the original strings remain unchanged. This immutability has both advantages and drawbacks.

The String Concatenation Operator (+)

The + operator is convenient for combining strings. For example:

```
String firstName = "John";
String lastName = "Doe";
String fullName = firstName + " " + lastName;
```

However, there are limitations to using + for string concatenation, especially when dealing with large numbers of concatenations.

Performance Pitfall

When concatenating strings using +, the cost increases significantly as the number of iterations grows. Each concatenation creates a new string, leading to memory overhead and garbage collection. Consider the following example:

```
String result = "";
for (int i = 0; i < 1000; i++) {
   result += " " + i;
}
```

In this loop, a new string is created in each iteration, resulting in poor performance.

The Solution: StringBuilder

To avoid performance issues, use StringBuilder for efficient string concatenation. StringBuilder allows mutable string building without unnecessary copies. Here's how you can rewrite the previous example:

```
StringBuilder builder = new StringBuilder();
for (int i = 0; i < 1000; i++) {
   builder.append(" ").append(i);
}
String result = builder.toString();
```

By using StringBuilder, you minimize memory allocation and achieve better performance.

Remember:

- For a **static number of strings**, using + is acceptable.
- In **loops**, prefer StringBuilder for better performance.

String Concatenation Operator (+)

The + operator is commonly used for combining strings in Java. It allows you to create a new string by joining two or more existing strings. For example:

```
String firstName = "John";
String lastName = "Doe";
String fullName = firstName + " " + lastName;
```

However, there are important considerations to keep in mind:

1. **Performance Overhead**: When using + for string concatenation, especially within loops, performance can suffer significantly. Each concatenation creates a new string object, leading to memory allocation and garbage collection overhead.

2. **Immutable Strings**: Strings in Java are immutable, meaning they cannot be modified after creation. When you concatenate strings using +, a new string is created, leaving the original strings unchanged. This immutability has both advantages and drawbacks.

3. **Compiler Optimization**: Modern Java compilers may optimize simple concatenations, but complex expressions or loops can still impact performance.

The Solution: StringBuilder

To avoid performance pitfalls, consider using StringBuilder for efficient string building. StringBuilder allows mutable string manipulation without unnecessary copies. Here's how you can rewrite the previous example using StringBuilder:

```
StringBuilder builder = new StringBuilder();
for (int i = 0; i < 1000; i++) {
   builder.append(" ").append(i);
}
String result = builder.toString();
```

By using StringBuilder, you minimize memory allocation and achieve better performance when concatenating strings.

Remember:

- For a **static number of strings**, using + is acceptable.
- In **loops**, prefer StringBuilder for improved performance.

String Concatenation Operator (+)

The + operator is commonly used for combining strings in Java. It allows you to create a new string by joining two or more existing strings. For example:

```
String firstName = "John";
String lastName = "Doe";
String fullName = firstName + " " + lastName;
```

However, there are important considerations to keep in mind:

1. **Performance Overhead**: When using + for string concatenation, especially within loops, performance can suffer significantly. Each concatenation creates a new string object, leading to memory allocation and garbage collection overhead.

2. **Immutable Strings**: Strings in Java are immutable, meaning they cannot be modified after creation. When you concatenate strings using +, a new string is created, leaving the original strings unchanged. This immutability has both advantages and drawbacks.

3. **Compiler Optimization**: Modern Java compilers may optimize simple concatenations, but complex expressions or loops can still impact performance.

The Solution: StringBuilder

To avoid performance pitfalls, consider using StringBuilder for efficient string building. StringBuilder allows mutable string manipulation without unnecessary copies. Here's how you can rewrite the previous example using StringBuilder:

```
StringBuilder builder = new StringBuilder();
for (int i = 0; i < 1000; i++) {
   builder.append(" ").append(i);
}
String result = builder.toString();
```

By using StringBuilder, you minimize memory allocation and achieve better performance when concatenating strings.

Remember:

- For a **static number of strings**, using + is acceptable.
- In **loops**, prefer StringBuilder for improved performance.

String Copies and Memory Overhead

When you concatenate strings using the + operator, each concatenation creates a new string object. This behavior can lead to memory overhead and negatively impact performance. Here's why:

1. **Immutability of Strings**: In Java, strings are immutable. Once created, a string cannot be modified. When you concatenate two strings using +, a new string is produced, leaving the original strings unchanged. This immutability has both advantages (such as thread safety) and drawbacks (such as performance implications).

2. **Memory Allocation**: Each concatenation operation allocates memory for the new string. If you perform many concatenations within a loop, memory usage can grow significantly. For example:

```
String result = "";
for (int i = 0; i < 1000; i++) {
   result += " " + i;
}
```

   In this loop, a new string is created in each iteration, resulting in unnecessary memory allocations.

3. **Garbage Collection**: Frequent string creations lead to more objects in memory, which triggers garbage collection. Garbage collection can be resource-intensive and impact overall application performance.

The Solution: StringBuilder

To address these issues, use StringBuilder for efficient string concatenation, especially within loops. StringBuilder provides mutable string building without unnecessary copies. Here's how you can rewrite the previous example:

```
StringBuilder builder = new StringBuilder();
for (int i = 0; i < 1000; i++) {
   builder.append(" ").append(i);
}
String result = builder.toString();
```

By using StringBuilder, you minimize memory allocation and achieve better performance. Remember:

- For a **static number of strings**, using + is acceptable.
- In **loops**, prefer StringBuilder for improved performance.

- ## Best Practices for Naming in Java: Adhering to Conventions

Introduction to Naming Conventions:

In the world of software development, **consistent naming** plays a crucial role in enhancing code readability and maintainability. When developers adhere to well-established naming conventions, it becomes easier for them to understand each other's code and collaborate effectively. In this article, we'll delve into the importance of naming conventions and explore the specific guidelines for naming in Java.

Java Naming Conventions:

Java has a set of **standard naming rules** that apply to various elements within your code. These conventions help maintain uniformity and make code more predictable. Let's take a closer look at these rules:

1. **Variables and Fields:**

   - Use **camelCase** for variable names (e.g., userName, totalAmount).
   - Start variable names with lowercase letters.
   - Be descriptive but concise.

2. **Methods:**

   - Use **camelCase** for method names (e.g., calculateTotal(), getUserInfo()).
   - Begin method names with verbs (e.g., get, set, compute).

3. **Classes and Interfaces:**

   - Use **PascalCase** (also known as **CamelCase with an initial uppercase letter**) for class and interface names (e.g., Customer, ProductService).
   - Class names should be nouns or noun phrases.

4. **Packages:**

   - Package names should be in **all lowercase**.
   - Use a reverse domain name as the package prefix (e.g., com.example.myapp).

Benefits of Using Standard Conventions:

Adhering to naming conventions offers several advantages:

- **Readability:** Consistent naming makes code easier to read and understand.
- **Collaboration:** When team members follow the same conventions, collaboration becomes smoother.
- **Avoiding Confusion:** Properly named identifiers reduce the chances of confusion and bugs.

Hungarian Notation and Its Pitfalls:

In the past, **Hungarian notation** was popular, where variable names included type information (e.g., strName, iCount). However, modern programming practices discourage its use. Why?

- **Redundancy:** Including type information in variable names duplicates information already available in the code.
- **Maintenance Nightmare:** As code evolves, updating type prefixes becomes cumbersome.

Effective Java Practices:

Joshua Bloch's book **"Effective Java"** emphasizes the importance of following Java conventions. Some key takeaways:

- **Be Descriptive:** Choose meaningful names that convey the purpose of the variable, method, or class.
- **Avoid Abbreviations:** Clear names are better than cryptic abbreviations.
- **Consistency Matters:** Stick to the conventions consistently throughout your project.

Remember, adhering to naming conventions isn't just about aesthetics—it directly impacts code quality and developer productivity. By following these best practices, you contribute to a cleaner, more maintainable codebase.

Let's dive deeper into **Java naming conventions** and explore the established rules for various elements within Java code. Additionally, I'll provide examples to illustrate how these conventions are applied to identifiers.

Variables and Fields:

1. **Variable Names:**

   - Use **camelCase** for variable names.
   - Start variable names with lowercase letters.
   - Be descriptive but concise.
   - Example: userName, totalAmount

2. **Fields (Class Variables):**

   - Similar to variables, use **camelCase** for field names.
   - Begin field names with lowercase letters.
   - Example: private int itemCount;

Methods:

1. **Method Names:**
   - Use **camelCase** for method names.
   - Begin method names with verbs (e.g., get, set, calculate).

- Example: public void calculateTotal()

Classes and Interfaces:

1. **Class Names:**

   - Use **PascalCase** (initial uppercase letter) for class names.
   - Class names should be nouns or noun phrases.
   - Example: public class Customer { ... }

2. **Interface Names:**

   - Also use **PascalCase** for interface names.
   - Prefix interface names with an "I" (if applicable).
   - Example: public interface ILogger { ... }

Packages:

1. **Package Names:**
   - Package names should be in **all lowercase**.
   - Use a reverse domain name as the package prefix.
   - Example: package com.example.myapp;

Examples:

- Variable: int itemCount = 10;
- Method: public String getUserName() { ... }
- Class: public class ProductService { ... }
- Interface: public interface IValidator { ... }

Remember, consistent adherence to these conventions enhances code readability and promotes better collaboration among developers.

Let's explore the benefits of adhering to language-specific conventions in software development, particularly in the context of Java:

Benefits of Using Standard Conventions

1. **Consistent Readability:**

   - Following naming conventions ensures that code is consistently readable across the entire project.
   - When everyone uses the same patterns for naming variables, methods, and classes, it becomes easier to understand the codebase.

2. **Collaboration and Teamwork:**

   - Consistent conventions simplify collaboration among team members.

- Developers can quickly grasp the purpose of identifiers without deciphering cryptic or inconsistent names.
- It fosters a sense of unity and shared understanding within the development team.

3. **Reduced Cognitive Load:**

   - Well-chosen names reduce cognitive load.
   - Developers spend less time trying to decipher the meaning of identifiers, allowing them to focus on solving actual problems.

4. **Avoidance of Ambiguity:**

   - Clear naming conventions minimize ambiguity.
   - When everyone follows the same rules, there's less room for interpretation.
   - Ambiguous names can lead to bugs and misunderstandings.

5. **Code Maintenance and Refactoring:**

   - During maintenance or refactoring, adhering to conventions simplifies the process.
   - Renaming variables or methods becomes straightforward because you know where to look and what to expect.

6. **Cross-Project Consistency:**

   - When working on multiple projects or collaborating with other teams, adhering to conventions ensures consistency.
   - It's easier to transition between projects when naming patterns remain the same.

7. **Avoiding "Religious Warfare":**

   - Without conventions, debates over naming styles can escalate into unnecessary conflicts.
   - Following established norms reduces the likelihood of heated discussions about code style.

Remember, naming conventions are not just about aesthetics; they significantly impact code quality, maintainability, and the overall development process. By embracing these conventions, developers contribute to a more efficient and harmonious coding environment.

Let's delve into the world of **Hungarian notation**, explore its pitfalls, and discuss effective Java practices for naming.

Hungarian Notation and Its Pitfalls

What is Hungarian Notation?

Hungarian Notation is a naming convention where variable names include type information as a prefix. For example:

- strName for a string variable
- iCount for an integer variable

The Pitfalls of Hungarian Notation:

1. **Redundancy:**

   - Including type information in variable names duplicates what's already evident from the variable's declaration.
   - Modern programming languages provide strong type systems, making explicit type prefixes unnecessary.

2. **Maintenance Nightmare:**

   - As code evolves, updating type prefixes becomes cumbersome.
   - Renaming variables requires changing both the name and the type prefix, leading to potential errors.

3. **Lack of Clarity:**

   - Hungarian notation can confuse developers who are not familiar with the specific prefixes.
   - It doesn't necessarily improve code readability; instead, it adds noise.

4. **Language Agnostic Issues:**

   - Hungarian notation originated in the C language, but it doesn't translate well to other languages.
   - In languages like Java, where type information is less critical, it's better to avoid this convention.

Java Practices

Joshua Bloch's "Effective Java"

Joshua Bloch's book, **"Effective Java"**, provides valuable insights into writing robust and maintainable Java code. Here are some relevant practices:

1. **Be Descriptive:**

   - Choose meaningful names that convey the purpose of the variable, method, or class.
   - Avoid cryptic abbreviations and overly short names.

2. **Consistency Matters:**

   - Stick to the established Java naming conventions.
   - Consistency across the codebase enhances readability.

3. **Avoid Hungarian Notation:**

   - Bloch advises against using Hungarian notation.
   - Trust the type system and let the code speak for itself.

Real-World Examples

Let's see how adhering to conventions improves code clarity:

```
// Before:
int iCount; // Hungarian notation
String strName; // Hungarian notation

// After:
int itemCount; // Clear and descriptive
String userName; // Meaningful and consistent
```

Remember, good naming practices contribute to maintainable code. So, embrace conventions, avoid Hungarian notation, and create code that speaks clearly to fellow developers!

Let's craft an article with the title **"Unlocking Java's Power: The Art of Interface Mastery"**. In this article, we'll explore the effective use of interfaces in Java, focusing on the following topics:

1. Why Prefer Interfaces?

When it comes to designing robust and flexible software, interfaces play a pivotal role. Here, we'll delve into the advantages of using interfaces over concrete classes:

- **Flexibility**: Interfaces allow you to define contracts that multiple classes can adhere to. This flexibility enables you to swap implementations seamlessly without affecting the rest of your codebase.
- **Maintainability**: By programming to interfaces, you create a clear separation between the contract (interface) and its implementations. This separation simplifies maintenance and updates.
- **Code Reusability**: Interfaces encourage reusable code. A single interface can be implemented by various classes, promoting efficient sharing of behavior across different components.

2. Referring to Objects by Their Interfaces: Best Practices

In this section, we'll explore the art of referring to objects by their interface types:

- **Interface-Based References**: Learn why it's beneficial to use interface types (e.g., List, Map, etc.) when interacting with objects. We'll provide practical examples to illustrate this practice.
- **Decoupling Components**: Discover how interface-based references enhance decoupling. When you refer to objects by their interfaces, you reduce dependencies and improve overall system design.

3. Contract and Behavior: The Interface Perspective

Interfaces not only define contracts but also encapsulate behavior. Here's what we'll cover:

- **Major Functionality**: Explore cases where an interface represents a significant functionality or purpose. We'll discuss real-world examples, such as collection classes and JDBC RowSet.
- **Specification Clarity**: Interfaces serve as clear specifications for implementing classes. We'll emphasize the importance of adhering to these contracts.

4. Interface vs. Abstract Class: When to Choose Which?

Finally, let's address the eternal debate: interface or abstract class?

- **Use Cases**: Compare interfaces and abstract classes based on their use cases. When should you opt for one over the other?
- **Trade-offs**: We'll weigh the pros and cons, helping you make informed decisions during your design process.

Remember, mastering interfaces unlocks the true potential of Java development. So, let's dive in and harness their power!

Let's dive into the best practices for referring to objects by their interface types in Java. By adhering to this principle, we can create more robust and maintainable code. Here are the key points:

1. Emphasizing Interface-Based References

When working with objects, prefer referring to them by their interface types rather than specific concrete implementations. Here's why:

- **Flexibility**: By using interfaces, you decouple your code from specific implementations. This flexibility allows you to switch out implementations without affecting other parts of your system.
- **Abstraction**: Interfaces provide an abstraction layer. When you interact with an object through its interface, you focus on the contract (methods and behavior) rather than implementation details.
- **Polymorphism**: Interface-based references enable polymorphism. You can treat different objects that implement the same interface interchangeably, enhancing code reusability.

2. Examples of Interface Types

Let's explore some common examples of using interface types:

- **List Interface**:
    - Instead of directly using ArrayList or LinkedList, declare variables as List<String> or List<Integer>. This allows you to switch between list implementations seamlessly.
    - Example:

        List<String> names = new ArrayList<>(); // Good practice

- **Map Interface**:
    - Use Map instead of specific map implementations like HashMap or TreeMap.
    - Example:

        Map<String, Integer> wordCount = new HashMap<>(); // Preferred

3. Scenarios for Interface-Based References

Consider the following scenarios where adhering to interface-based references improves code design:

- **Dependency Injection (DI)**:
    - DI frameworks rely heavily on interfaces. By injecting dependencies via interfaces, you achieve loose coupling and better testability.

- **API Design**:
  - When designing APIs, expose interfaces rather than concrete classes. This allows clients to interact with your API through well-defined contracts.
- **Unit Testing**:
  - In unit tests, mock objects are often created using interfaces. This isolates the tested component from its dependencies.

Remember, embracing interface-based references promotes cleaner, more modular code. So, next time you're tempted to use concrete implementations directly, think interfaces first!

Let's delve into the fascinating world of interfaces and their impact on code design.

Contract and Behavior: The Interface Perspective

1. Major Functionality and Purpose

Interfaces often encapsulate major functionality or serve as blueprints for specific behaviors. Here's how:

- **Collection Framework**:
  - The Java Collection Framework relies heavily on interfaces. For instance:
    - List: Represents an ordered collection with duplicates allowed.
    - Set: Represents a collection with no duplicates.
    - Map: Represents key-value pairs.
  - By adhering to these interfaces, developers can create custom implementations (e.g., ArrayList, HashSet, HashMap) that fulfill the expected behavior.
- **JDBC (Java Database Connectivity)**:
  - JDBC provides a standard interface for connecting to databases. The java.sql package defines key interfaces:
    - Connection: Represents a database connection.
    - Statement: Represents an SQL statement.
    - ResultSet: Represents the result of a query.
  - Implementations (e.g., OracleConnection, PreparedStatement) adhere to these contracts, allowing seamless interaction with various databases.

2. Defining Contracts and Specifications

Interfaces define clear contracts that implementing classes must adhere to:

- **Method Signatures**:
  - An interface specifies method signatures without implementation details.

- Example:

```
public interface Shape {
    double area();
    double perimeter();
}
```

- **Implementing the Contract**:

  - Any class implementing Shape must provide concrete implementations for area() and perimeter().
  - This ensures consistency across different shapes (e.g., circles, rectangles) while allowing custom behavior.

3. Real-World Examples

Let's explore practical scenarios where interface-based references make sense:

- **Dependency Injection (DI)**:

  - DI frameworks (e.g., Spring) rely on interfaces to inject dependencies.
  - Example:

```
@Autowired
private UserRepository userRepository; // UserRepository implements CRUD operations
```

- **Custom File Readers/Writers**:

  - Suppose you need to read/write data from/to different file formats (e.g., CSV, XML, JSON).
  - Define an interface (FileReader, FileWriter) with methods like read() and write().
  - Implementations handle specific formats (e.g., CsvFileReader, JsonFileWriter).

- **Plugin Systems**:

  - Interfaces enable extensible plugin architectures.
  - A core system defines an interface, and plugins implement it.
  - Example: A text editor with spell-check plugins adhering to an SpellChecker interface.

Remember, interfaces provide a powerful way to express contracts and behavior. They guide developers, promote consistency, and foster collaboration across different components.

Let's delve into the comparison between interfaces and abstract classes in Java, exploring their use cases, preferences, and trade-offs.

Interface vs. Abstract Class: When to Choose Which?

1. Use Cases and Definitions

- **Interfaces**:

    - **Definition**: An interface defines a contract that a class must adhere to. It specifies method signatures without implementation details.
    - **Use Cases**:
        - When you want to define a common contract for unrelated classes.
        - When multiple classes need to provide the same set of methods (e.g., Comparable, Serializable).
        - When achieving multiple inheritance-like behavior (since Java doesn't support multiple inheritance of classes).

- **Abstract Classes**:

    - **Definition**: An abstract class is a class that cannot be instantiated directly. It can contain both abstract (unimplemented) methods and concrete (implemented) methods.
    - **Use Cases**:
        - When you want to provide a base class with some common functionality for its subclasses.
        - When you need to share code among related classes.
        - When you want to enforce certain methods to be implemented by subclasses.

2. Scenarios Favoring Interfaces

- **Flexibility and Decoupling**:

    - **Interfaces**: By programming to interfaces, you achieve loose coupling. Clients interact with objects through interfaces, allowing easy substitution of implementations.
    - **Example**: Dependency injection frameworks rely heavily on interfaces for injecting dependencies.

- **Multiple Inheritance-Like Behavior**:

    - **Interfaces**: Java doesn't support multiple inheritance of classes, but it allows implementing multiple interfaces. Use interfaces to achieve behavior from multiple sources.
    - **Example**: A class implementing both Runnable and Serializable.

- **API Design and Contracts**:

    - **Interfaces**: When designing APIs, expose interfaces rather than concrete classes. This defines clear contracts for clients.

- **Example**: The Java Collection Framework (e.g., List, Set, Map) provides consistent behavior through interfaces.

3. Trade-Offs and Considerations

- **Abstract Classes**:

    - **Pros**:
        - Can provide default implementations (concrete methods).
        - Allow shared state (instance variables).
        - Can enforce method implementation (abstract methods).
    - **Cons**:
        - Tighter coupling (subclasses inherit implementation details).
        - Limits inheritance (only single inheritance allowed).
- **Interfaces**:

    - **Pros**:
        - Promote flexibility and decoupling.
        - Support multiple inheritance-like behavior.
        - Clear contracts.
    - **Cons**:
        - No default implementations (until Java 8's default methods).
        - No shared state (only constants allowed).
        - No constructors.

4. Making the Choice

- **Choose Abstract Classes When**:

    - You want to provide a common base class with shared functionality.
    - You need to enforce method implementation.
    - You're dealing with related classes.
- **Choose Interfaces When**:

    - You want to define contracts without implementation.
    - You need flexibility and multiple inheritance-like behavior.
    - You're designing APIs or handling unrelated classes.

Remember, both interfaces and abstract classes have their place in Java development. Consider your specific requirements and design accordingly!

• Use Exceptions Only for Exceptional Conditions

Exception handling is a crucial aspect of writing robust and reliable code in Java. However, it's essential to use exceptions appropriately to maintain code clarity and avoid common pitfalls. In this article, we'll explore why you should limit exceptions to truly exceptional scenarios and avoid using them for regular control flow.

1. The Purpose of Exceptions

Exceptions serve as a mechanism to handle unexpected and exceptional situations during program execution. They allow you to gracefully handle errors, propagate information about failures, and ensure proper resource cleanup. However, their misuse can lead to confusing code and performance issues.

2. The Anti-Pattern: Using Exceptions for Control Flow

2.1. The Strange Form of Logic

Consider the following code snippet:

```java
public void run() {
   MyException ex = null;
   while (ex == null) {
     try {
        // Do stuff
     } catch (MyException e) {
        // Maybe handle this exception
        ex = e;
     }
   }
}
```

This construct uses exceptions as a form of control flow. It checks whether the exception MyException has been thrown and continues looping until it's caught. While technically possible, this approach is unconventional and harder to read.

2.2. Simplifying the Logic

A more straightforward alternative is:

```java
public void run() {
   while (true) {
     try {
        // Do stuff
     } catch (MyException e) {
        // Maybe handle this exception
        break;
     }
   }
}
```

Here, we use an infinite loop and break out when the exception occurs. It's cleaner and easier to understand.

2.3. Propagating Exceptions

If your method signature already declares throws MyException, you can let the exception propagate to the caller:

```
public void run() throws MyException {
    while (true) {
        // Or maybe some exit condition?
        try {
            // Do stuff
        } catch (MyException e) {
            // Maybe handle this exception
        }
    }
}
```

The caller can then handle the exception appropriately.

3. Best Practices

- **Use Exceptions Sparingly**: Reserve exceptions for truly exceptional conditions, such as unexpected errors or resource unavailability.
- **Avoid Flow Control with Exceptions**: Don't rely on exceptions for regular program flow. Use them only when necessary.
- **Read Effective Java**: Item 57 in *Effective Java* by Joshua Bloch emphasizes this principle.

Remember, exceptions are powerful tools, but their misuse can lead to code that's hard to maintain and debug. Use them wisely, and your Java code will be more robust and maintainable.

1. Checked Exceptions

Checked exceptions are a category of exceptions that the compiler mandates you to handle explicitly. They typically represent **recoverable conditions**—situations where your program can take corrective action. Here are some key points about checked exceptions:

- **Examples**: IOException, SQLException, FileNotFoundException, etc.
- **Handling Requirement**: You must either catch them using a try-catch block or declare them in the method signature using the throws clause.
- **Use Cases**:
    - File I/O operations (e.g., reading from a file).
    - Database interactions (e.g., connecting to a database).
    - Network communication (e.g., handling socket exceptions).
- **Best Practices**:
    - Handle checked exceptions gracefully by providing meaningful error messages or logging.
    - Consider wrapping checked exceptions in custom application-specific exceptions for better abstraction.

2. Runtime Exceptions (Unchecked Exceptions)

Runtime exceptions (also known as unchecked exceptions) do not require explicit handling. They represent **programming errors**—issues that should ideally be fixed during development. Key points about runtime exceptions:

- **Examples**: NullPointerException, ArrayIndexOutOfBoundsException, IllegalArgumentException, etc.
- **Handling Requirement**: No explicit handling is enforced by the compiler.
- **Use Cases**:
    - Accessing null references.
    - Indexing an array out of bounds.
    - Passing invalid arguments to methods.
- **Best Practices**:
    - Prevent runtime exceptions by writing robust code.
    - Validate inputs and avoid null references.
    - Use appropriate data structures and algorithms to avoid index-related issues.

3. Choosing Wisely

When designing your Java application, consider the following guidelines:

- **Use Checked Exceptions When**:
    - The error is recoverable.

- You want to force the caller to handle the exception explicitly.
- The exception is part of the expected flow of your application.
- **Use Runtime Exceptions When**:

    - The error is due to programming mistakes.
    - You want to avoid cluttering your code with excessive try-catch blocks.
    - The exception indicates a bug that needs fixing.

Remember, both checked and runtime exceptions have their place in Java, and understanding when to use each type is essential for writing clean, maintainable code.

Let's delve into the topic of **avoiding unnecessary use of checked exceptions** in Java.

• Avoid Unnecessary Use of Checked Exceptions

1. The Purpose of Checked Exceptions

Java provides two main categories of exceptions: **checked exceptions** and **unchecked exceptions** (also known as runtime exceptions). Checked exceptions are those that the compiler mandates you to handle explicitly. They typically represent **recoverable conditions**—situations where your program can take corrective action.

2. The Problem with Overusing Checked Exceptions

While checked exceptions serve a valuable purpose, their misuse can lead to code that is harder to read, maintain, and reason about. Here are some common issues associated with excessive use of checked exceptions:

- **Painful API Usage**: When an API throws numerous checked exceptions, it becomes cumbersome for callers to handle them all.

- **Code Clutter**: Excessive try-catch blocks clutter the code, making it less readable. When every method call potentially throws multiple checked exceptions, the code becomes verbose and less expressive.

3. Guidelines for Using Checked Exceptions

To avoid unnecessary use of checked exceptions, consider the following best practices:

- **Reserve Checked Exceptions for Recoverable Conditions**: Only use checked exceptions for scenarios where the caller can reasonably recover from the error. If the caller cannot do anything meaningful to handle the exception, reconsider whether it should be checked.

- **Avoid Checked Exceptions for Unrecoverable Situations**: If an exception represents a condition from which the caller could not possibly recover, or if the only foreseeable response would be for the program to exit, it's better to use an unchecked exception (runtime exception) instead.

- **Effective Java Item 41**: Joshua Bloch's *Effective Java* recommends avoiding unnecessary checked exceptions. Keep this principle in mind when designing your APIs.

4. Wrapping Checked Exceptions

In some cases, you might encounter third-party libraries or APIs that throw checked exceptions excessively. To mitigate this, consider wrapping checked exceptions in custom application-specific exceptions. This way, you can provide a higher-level abstraction and simplify the API usage for your callers.

Remember, the goal is to strike a balance between providing meaningful error handling and avoiding unnecessary complexity. By using checked exceptions judiciously, you can create cleaner, more maintainable code.

Let's discuss the importance of **not ignoring exceptions** in Java.

• Please Don't Ignore Exceptions: A Guide to Exception Handling in Java

Exception handling is a critical aspect of writing reliable and robust Java code. Ignoring exceptions can lead to unexpected behavior, obscure bugs, and compromised system stability. In this article, we'll explore why you should never turn a blind eye to exceptions and how to handle them effectively.

1. The Consequences of Ignoring Exceptions

When you ignore exceptions, several problems arise:

- **Silent Failures**: Ignored exceptions silently fail without providing any indication of what went wrong. This lack of feedback can make debugging challenging.

- **Resource Leaks**: Exceptions often occur during resource management (e.g., file I/O, database connections). Ignoring them can lead to resource leaks, leaving files unclosed or connections dangling.

- **Unpredictable Behavior**: Ignored exceptions can cause unpredictable behavior. Your program might continue executing in an inconsistent state, leading to unexpected results.

2. Best Practices for Exception Handling

2.1. Catch and Handle Exceptions

Always catch exceptions explicitly using try-catch blocks. Handle exceptions gracefully by providing meaningful error messages or logging relevant information. Even if you can't recover immediately, logging the exception helps diagnose issues later.

2.2. Log Exceptions

Logging exceptions is crucial. Use a logging framework (e.g., Log4j, SLF4J) to record exception details. Include information like the exception type, stack trace, and context. Proper logging aids in troubleshooting and identifying root causes.

2.3. Avoid Empty Catch Blocks

Empty catch blocks (e.g., catch (Exception e) {}) are dangerous. At the very least, log the exception. If you decide not to handle it immediately, someone else might need that information later.

2.4. Use Unchecked Exceptions Wisely

Unchecked exceptions (runtime exceptions) don't require explicit handling. However, use them judiciously. They indicate programming errors (e.g., null references, array index out of bounds) and should be fixed during development.

3. Effective Java's Advice

Joshua Bloch's *Effective Java* provides valuable guidance on exception handling:

- **Item 40**: "Use checked exceptions for recoverable conditions and runtime exceptions for programming errors."
- **Item 41**: "Avoid unnecessary use of checked exceptions." Only use checked exceptions when the caller can reasonably recover from the error.

4. Wrapping Up

Remember, robust exception handling is essential for writing maintainable and reliable Java applications. Don't ignore exceptions—treat them as valuable feedback from your code, and handle them appropriately.

- **About the author**

Edson L. P. Camacho: Bridging Creativity and Technology

Edson L. P. Camacho is a highly accomplished professional with a passion for both technology and creativity. His educational background includes a degree in **Technology in Digital Games** from UniCV in Brazil, as well as a postgraduate degree in **Artificial Intelligence with a focus on Software Engineering**.

Expertise and Impact:

1. **Game Development Mentor**:

   - Edson's extensive experience in teaching and mentoring has positively impacted the lives of hundreds of students. He has guided aspiring game developers through the intricacies of creating digital games using tools such as **Unity, C#**, and the **Unreal Engine**.
   - His patient and insightful approach empowers students to unlock their creative potential and build engaging, interactive experiences.

2. **Beyond Game Development**:

   - Edson's curiosity extends beyond game development. He is an avid student of **digital painting** and **3D modeling** for games. By immersing himself in these artistic disciplines, he gains a deeper understanding of aesthetics and visual storytelling.
   - This holistic approach allows him to create well-rounded content and inspire others to explore the intersection of technology and art.

3. **Cutting-Edge Innovator**:

   - Edson thrives on pushing boundaries. He constantly explores the latest technologies and techniques, seeking novel solutions to complex problems.
   - Whether it's leveraging **Lambda expressions**, mastering **stream processing**, or diving into **generics**, Edson remains at the forefront of industry advancements.

4. **Unwavering Commitment**:

   - Edson's dedication to his students and the field of digital game development is unwavering. His passion fuels his mission to elevate the skills of aspiring developers.
   - As an invaluable resource, he encourages others to embrace continuous learning and strive for excellence.

In summary, Edson L. P. Camacho embodies the fusion of creativity and technology. His journey is an inspiration to all who seek to create, innovate, and leave a lasting impact in the ever-evolving world of software development.

One day the prophet Isaiah said...

"All men are like grass and all their glory is like the flowers of the field... The grass withers and the flowers fall, but the Word of our God stands forever."

Isaiah 40: 7-8

www.ingramcontent.com/pod-product-compliance
Lightning Source LLC
Chambersburg PA
CBHW080525060326
40690CB00022B/5028